50% OF

Online PELLETB Prep Course!

By Mometrix

Dear Customer,

We consider it an honor and a privilege that you chose our PELLETB Study Guide. As a way of showing our appreciation and to help us better serve you, we are offering **50% off our online PELLETB Prep Course**. Many PELLETB courses are needlessly expensive and don't deliver enough value. With our course, you get access to the best PELLETB prep material, and **you only pay half price**.

We have structured our online course to perfectly complement your printed study guide. The PELLETB Prep Course contains **in-depth lessons** that cover all the most important topics, **30+ video reviews** that explain difficult concepts, and over **900 practice questions** to ensure you feel prepared so you can study while you're on the go.

Online PELLETB Prep Course

Topics Included:

- Writing Ability
    - Clarity
    - Spelling
    - Vocabulary
- Reading Ability
    - Reading Comprehension
    - Cloze Test
- Reasoning Ability
    - Comparative Values
    - Numerical Series
    - Similar Words

Course Features:

- PELLETB Study Guide
    - Get content that complements our best-selling study guide.
- Full-Length Practice Tests
    - With over 900 practice questions, you can test yourself again and again.
- Mobile Friendly
    - If you need to study on the go, the course is easily accessible from your mobile device.

To receive this discount, visit us at mometrix.com/university/pelletb or simply scan this QR code with your smartphone. At the checkout page, enter the discount code: **pellb50off**

If you have any questions or concerns, please contact us at support@mometrix.com.

FREE Study Skills Videos/DVD Offer

Dear Customer,

Thank you for your purchase from Mometrix! We consider it an honor and a privilege that you have purchased our product and we want to ensure your satisfaction.

As part of our ongoing effort to meet the needs of test takers, we have developed a set of Study Skills Videos that we would like to give you for FREE. These videos cover our *best practices* for getting ready for your exam, from how to use our study materials to how to best prepare for the day of the test.

All that we ask is that you email us with feedback that would describe your experience so far with our product. Good, bad, or indifferent, we want to know what you think!

To get your FREE Study Skills Videos, you can use the **QR code** below, or send us an **email** at studyvideos@mometrix.com with *FREE VIDEOS* in the subject line and the following information in the body of the email:

- The name of the product you purchased.
- Your product rating on a scale of 1-5, with 5 being the highest rating.
- Your feedback. It can be long, short, or anything in between. We just want to know your impressions and experience so far with our product. (Good feedback might include how our study material met your needs and ways we might be able to make it even better. You could highlight features that you found helpful or features that you think we should add.)

If you have any questions or concerns, please don't hesitate to contact me directly.

Thanks again!

Sincerely,

Jay Willis
Vice President
jay.willis@mometrix.com
1-800-673-8175

PELLET B Secrets

Study Guide
Your Key to Exam Success

- California POST Exam Secrets Study Guide
- 4 Full-Length Practice Tests
- Step-by-Step Review Video Tutorials for the California Police Officer Exam

Written and edited by the Mometrix Test Prep

Printed in the United States of America

This paper meets the requirements of ANSI/NISO Z39.48-1992 (Permanence of Paper).

Paperback
ISBN 13: 978-1-5167-1061-4
ISBN 10: 1-51671-061-4

Ebook
ISBN 13: 978-1-5167-1719-4
ISBN 10: 1-5167-1719-8

Hardback
ISBN 13: 978-1-5167-1394-3
ISBN 10: 1-5167-1394-X

Dear Future Exam Success Story

First of all, **THANK YOU** for purchasing Mometrix study materials!

Second, congratulations! You are one of the few determined test-takers who are committed to doing whatever it takes to excel on your exam. **You have come to the right place.** We developed these study materials with one goal in mind: to deliver you the information you need in a format that's concise and easy to use.

In addition to optimizing your guide for the content of the test, we've outlined our recommended steps for breaking down the preparation process into small, attainable goals so you can make sure you stay on track.

We've also analyzed the entire test-taking process, identifying the most common pitfalls and showing how you can overcome them and be ready for any curveball the test throws you.

Standardized testing is one of the biggest obstacles on your road to success, which only increases the importance of doing well in the high-pressure, high-stakes environment of test day. Your results on this test could have a significant impact on your future, and this guide provides the information and practical advice to help you achieve your full potential on test day.

Your success is our success

We would love to hear from you! If you would like to share the story of your exam success or if you have any questions or comments in regard to our products, please contact us at **800-673-8175** or **support@mometrix.com**.

Thanks again for your business and we wish you continued success!

Sincerely,
The Mometrix Test Preparation Team

Table of Contents

Introduction

Thank you for purchasing this resource! You have made the choice to prepare yourself for a test that could have a huge impact on your future, and this guide is designed to help you be fully ready for test day. Obviously, it's important to have a solid understanding of the test material, but you also need to be prepared for the unique environment and stressors of the test, so that you can perform to the best of your abilities.

For this purpose, the first section that appears in this guide is the **Secret Keys**. We've devoted countless hours to meticulously researching what works and what doesn't, and we've boiled down our findings to the five most impactful steps you can take to improve your performance on the test. We start at the beginning with study planning and move through the preparation process, all the way to the testing strategies that will help you get the most out of what you know when you're finally sitting in front of the test.

We recommend that you start preparing for your test as far in advance as possible. However, if you've bought this guide as a last-minute study resource and only have a few days before your test, we recommend that you skip over the first two Secret Keys since they address a long-term study plan.

If you struggle with **test anxiety**, we strongly encourage you to check out our recommendations for how you can overcome it. Test anxiety is a formidable foe, but it can be beaten, and we want to make sure you have the tools you need to defeat it.

Review Video Directory

As you work your way through this guide, you will see numerous review video links interspersed with the written content. If you would like to access all of these review videos in one place, click on the video directory link found on the bonus page: **mometrix.com/bonus948/pelletb**

Secret Key #1 – Plan Big, Study Small

There's a lot riding on your performance. If you want to ace this test, you're going to need to keep your skills sharp and the material fresh in your mind. You need a plan that lets you review everything you need to know while still fitting in your schedule. We'll break this strategy down into three categories.

Information Organization

Start with the information you already have: the official test outline. From this, you can make a complete list of all the concepts you need to cover before the test. Organize these concepts into groups that can be studied together, and create a list of any related vocabulary you need to learn so you can brush up on any difficult terms. You'll want to keep this vocabulary list handy once you actually start studying since you may need to add to it along the way.

Time Management

Once you have your set of study concepts, decide how to spread them out over the time you have left before the test. Break your study plan into small, clear goals so you have a manageable task for each day and know exactly what you're doing. Then just focus on one small step at a time. When you manage your time this way, you don't need to spend hours at a time studying. Studying a small block of content for a short period each day helps you retain information better and avoid stressing over how much you have left to do. You can relax knowing that you have a plan to cover everything in time. In order for this strategy to be effective though, you have to start studying early and stick to your schedule. Avoid the exhaustion and futility that comes from last-minute cramming!

Study Environment

The environment you study in has a big impact on your learning. Studying in a coffee shop, while probably more enjoyable, is not likely to be as fruitful as studying in a quiet room. It's important to keep distractions to a minimum. You're only planning to study for a short block of time, so make the most of it. Don't pause to check your phone or get up to find a snack. It's also important to **avoid multitasking**. Research has consistently shown that multitasking will make your studying dramatically less effective. Your study area should also be comfortable and well-lit so you don't have the distraction of straining your eyes or sitting on an uncomfortable chair.

The time of day you study is also important. You want to be rested and alert. Don't wait until just before bedtime. Study when you'll be most likely to comprehend and remember. Even better, if you know what time of day your test will be, set that time aside for study. That way your brain will be used to working on that subject at that specific time and you'll have a better chance of recalling information.

Finally, it can be helpful to team up with others who are studying for the same test. Your actual studying should be done in as isolated an environment as possible, but the work of organizing the information and setting up the study plan can be divided up. In between study sessions, you can discuss with your teammates the concepts that you're all studying and quiz each other on the details. Just be sure that your teammates are as serious about the test as you are. If you find that your study time is being replaced with social time, you might need to find a new team.

Secret Key #2 – Make Your Studying Count

You're devoting a lot of time and effort to preparing for this test, so you want to be absolutely certain it will pay off. This means doing more than just reading the content and hoping you can remember it on test day. It's important to make every minute of study count. There are two main areas you can focus on to make your studying count.

Retention

It doesn't matter how much time you study if you can't remember the material. You need to make sure you are retaining the concepts. To check your retention of the information you're learning, try recalling it at later times with minimal prompting. Try carrying around flashcards and glance at one or two from time to time or ask a friend who's also studying for the test to quiz you.

To enhance your retention, look for ways to put the information into practice so that you can apply it rather than simply recalling it. If you're using the information in practical ways, it will be much easier to remember. Similarly, it helps to solidify a concept in your mind if you're not only reading it to yourself but also explaining it to someone else. Ask a friend to let you teach them about a concept you're a little shaky on (or speak aloud to an imaginary audience if necessary). As you try to summarize, define, give examples, and answer your friend's questions, you'll understand the concepts better and they will stay with you longer. Finally, step back for a big picture view and ask yourself how each piece of information fits with the whole subject. When you link the different concepts together and see them working together as a whole, it's easier to remember the individual components.

Finally, practice showing your work on any multi-step problems, even if you're just studying. Writing out each step you take to solve a problem will help solidify the process in your mind, and you'll be more likely to remember it during the test.

Modality

Modality simply refers to the means or method by which you study. Choosing a study modality that fits your own individual learning style is crucial. No two people learn best in exactly the same way, so it's important to know your strengths and use them to your advantage.

For example, if you learn best by visualization, focus on visualizing a concept in your mind and draw an image or a diagram. Try color-coding your notes, illustrating them, or creating symbols that will trigger your mind to recall a learned concept. If you learn best by hearing or discussing information, find a study partner who learns the same way or read aloud to yourself. Think about how to put the information in your own words. Imagine that you are giving a lecture on the topic and record yourself so you can listen to it later.

For any learning style, flashcards can be helpful. Organize the information so you can take advantage of spare moments to review. Underline key words or phrases. Use different colors for different categories. Mnemonic devices (such as creating a short list in which every item starts with the same letter) can also help with retention. Find what works best for you and use it to store the information in your mind most effectively and easily.

Secret Key #3 – Practice the Right Way

Your success on test day depends not only on how many hours you put into preparing, but also on whether you prepared the right way. It's good to check along the way to see if your studying is paying off. One of the most effective ways to do this is by taking practice tests to evaluate your progress. Practice tests are useful because they show exactly where you need to improve. Every time you take a practice test, pay special attention to these three groups of questions:

- The questions you got wrong
- The questions you had to guess on, even if you guessed right
- The questions you found difficult or slow to work through

This will show you exactly what your weak areas are, and where you need to devote more study time. Ask yourself why each of these questions gave you trouble. Was it because you didn't understand the material? Was it because you didn't remember the vocabulary? Do you need more repetitions on this type of question to build speed and confidence? Dig into those questions and figure out how you can strengthen your weak areas as you go back to review the material.

Additionally, many practice tests have a section explaining the answer choices. It can be tempting to read the explanation and think that you now have a good understanding of the concept. However, an explanation likely only covers part of the question's broader context. Even if the explanation makes perfect sense, **go back and investigate** every concept related to the question until you're positive you have a thorough understanding.

As you go along, keep in mind that the practice test is just that: practice. Memorizing these questions and answers will not be very helpful on the actual test because it is unlikely to have any of the same exact questions. If you only know the right answers to the sample questions, you won't be prepared for the real thing. **Study the concepts** until you understand them fully, and then you'll be able to answer any question that shows up on the test.

It's important to wait on the practice tests until you're ready. If you take a test on your first day of study, you may be overwhelmed by the amount of material covered and how much you need to learn. Work up to it gradually.

On test day, you'll need to be prepared for answering questions, managing your time, and using the test-taking strategies you've learned. It's a lot to balance, like a mental marathon that will have a big impact on your future. Like training for a marathon, you'll need to start slowly and work your way up. When test day arrives, you'll be ready.

Start with the strategies you've read in the first two Secret Keys—plan your course and study in the way that works best for you. If you have time, consider using multiple study resources to get different approaches to the same concepts. It can be helpful to see difficult concepts from more than one angle. Then find a good source for practice tests. Many times, the test website will suggest potential study resources or provide sample tests.

Practice Test Strategy

If you're able to find at least three practice tests, we recommend this strategy:

Untimed and Open-Book Practice

Take the first test with no time constraints and with your notes and study guide handy. Take your time and focus on applying the strategies you've learned.

Timed and Open-Book Practice

Take the second practice test open-book as well, but set a timer and practice pacing yourself to finish in time.

Timed and Closed-Book Practice

Take any other practice tests as if it were test day. Set a timer and put away your study materials. Sit at a table or desk in a quiet room, imagine yourself at the testing center, and answer questions as quickly and accurately as possible.

Keep repeating timed and closed-book tests on a regular basis until you run out of practice tests or it's time for the actual test. Your mind will be ready for the schedule and stress of test day, and you'll be able to focus on recalling the material you've learned.

Secret Key #4 – Pace Yourself

Once you're fully prepared for the material on the test, your biggest challenge on test day will be managing your time. Just knowing that the clock is ticking can make you panic even if you have plenty of time left. Work on pacing yourself so you can build confidence against the time constraints of the exam. Pacing is a difficult skill to master, especially in a high-pressure environment, so **practice is vital**.

Set time expectations for your pace based on how much time is available. For example, if a section has 60 questions and the time limit is 30 minutes, you know you have to average 30 seconds or less per question in order to answer them all. Although 30 seconds is the hard limit, set 25 seconds per question as your goal, so you reserve extra time to spend on harder questions. When you budget extra time for the harder questions, you no longer have any reason to stress when those questions take longer to answer.

Don't let this time expectation distract you from working through the test at a calm, steady pace, but keep it in mind so you don't spend too much time on any one question. Recognize that taking extra time on one question you don't understand may keep you from answering two that you do understand later in the test. If your time limit for a question is up and you're still not sure of the answer, mark it and move on, and come back to it later if the time and the test format allow. If the testing format doesn't allow you to return to earlier questions, just make an educated guess; then put it out of your mind and move on.

On the easier questions, be careful not to rush. It may seem wise to hurry through them so you have more time for the challenging ones, but it's not worth missing one if you know the concept and just didn't take the time to read the question fully. Work efficiently but make sure you understand the question and have looked at all of the answer choices, since more than one may seem right at first.

Even if you're paying attention to the time, you may find yourself a little behind at some point. You should speed up to get back on track, but do so wisely. Don't panic; just take a few seconds less on each question until you're caught up. Don't guess without thinking, but do look through the answer choices and eliminate any you know are wrong. If you can get down to two choices, it is often worthwhile to guess from those. Once you've chosen an answer, move on and don't dwell on any that you skipped or had to hurry through. If a question was taking too long, chances are it was one of the harder ones, so you weren't as likely to get it right anyway.

On the other hand, if you find yourself getting ahead of schedule, it may be beneficial to slow down a little. The more quickly you work, the more likely you are to make a careless mistake that will affect your score. You've budgeted time for each question, so don't be afraid to spend that time. Practice an efficient but careful pace to get the most out of the time you have.

Secret Key #5 – Have a Plan for Guessing

When you're taking the test, you may find yourself stuck on a question. Some of the answer choices seem better than others, but you don't see the one answer choice that is obviously correct. What do you do?

The scenario described above is very common, yet most test takers have not effectively prepared for it. Developing and practicing a plan for guessing may be one of the single most effective uses of your time as you get ready for the exam.

In developing your plan for guessing, there are three questions to address:

- When should you start the guessing process?
- How should you narrow down the choices?
- Which answer should you choose?

When to Start the Guessing Process

Unless your plan for guessing is to select C every time (which, despite its merits, is not what we recommend), you need to leave yourself enough time to apply your answer elimination strategies. Since you have a limited amount of time for each question, that means that if you're going to give yourself the best shot at guessing correctly, you have to decide quickly whether or not you will guess.

Of course, the best-case scenario is that you don't have to guess at all, so first, see if you can answer the question based on your knowledge of the subject and basic reasoning skills. Focus on the key words in the question and try to jog your memory of related topics. Give yourself a chance to bring the knowledge to mind, but once you realize that you don't have (or you can't access) the knowledge you need to answer the question, it's time to start the guessing process.

It's almost always better to start the guessing process too early than too late. It only takes a few seconds to remember something and answer the question from knowledge. Carefully eliminating wrong answer choices takes longer. Plus, going through the process of eliminating answer choices can actually help jog your memory.

Summary: Start the guessing process as soon as you decide that you can't answer the question based on your knowledge.

How to Narrow Down the Choices

The next chapter in this book (**Test-Taking Strategies**) includes a wide range of strategies for how to approach questions and how to look for answer choices to eliminate. You will definitely want to read those carefully, practice them, and figure out which ones work best for you. Here though, we're going to address a mindset rather than a particular strategy.

Your odds of guessing an answer correctly depend on how many options you are choosing from.

Number of options left	5	4	3	2	1
Odds of guessing correctly	20%	25%	33%	50%	100%

You can see from this chart just how valuable it is to be able to eliminate incorrect answers and make an educated guess, but there are two things that many test takers do that cause them to miss out on the benefits of guessing:

- Accidentally eliminating the correct answer
- Selecting an answer based on an impression

We'll look at the first one here, and the second one in the next section.

To avoid accidentally eliminating the correct answer, we recommend a thought exercise called **the $5 challenge**. In this challenge, you only eliminate an answer choice from contention if you are willing to bet $5 on it being wrong. Why $5? Five dollars is a small but not insignificant amount of money. It's an amount you could afford to lose but wouldn't want to throw away. And while losing $5 once might not hurt too much, doing it twenty times will set you back $100. In the same way, each small decision you make—eliminating a choice here, guessing on a question there—won't by itself impact your score very much, but when you put them all together, they can make a big difference. By holding each answer choice elimination decision to a higher standard, you can reduce the risk of accidentally eliminating the correct answer.

The $5 challenge can also be applied in a positive sense: If you are willing to bet $5 that an answer choice *is* correct, go ahead and mark it as correct.

Summary: Only eliminate an answer choice if you are willing to bet $5 that it is wrong.

Which Answer to Choose

You're taking the test. You've run into a hard question and decided you'll have to guess. You've eliminated all the answer choices you're willing to bet $5 on. Now you have to pick an answer. Why do we even need to talk about this? Why can't you just pick whichever one you feel like when the time comes?

The answer to these questions is that if you don't come into the test with a plan, you'll rely on your impression to select an answer choice, and if you do that, you risk falling into a trap. The test writers know that everyone who takes their test will be guessing on some of the questions, so they intentionally write wrong answer choices to seem plausible. You still have to pick an answer though, and if the wrong answer choices are designed to look right, how can you ever be sure that you're not falling for their trap? The best solution we've found to this dilemma is to take the decision out of your hands entirely. Here is the process we recommend:

Once you've eliminated any choices that you are confident (willing to bet $5) are wrong, select the first remaining choice as your answer.

Whether you choose to select the first remaining choice, the second, or the last, the important thing is that you use some preselected standard. Using this approach guarantees that you will not be enticed into selecting an answer choice that looks right, because you are not basing your decision on how the answer choices look.

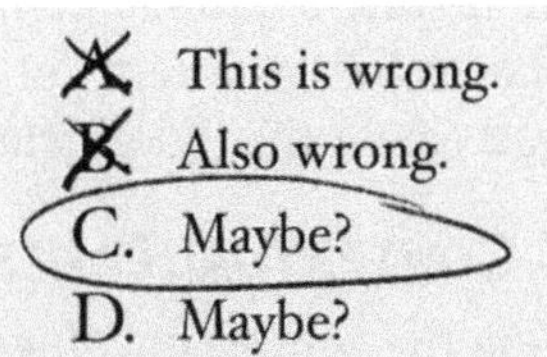

This is not meant to make you question your knowledge. Instead, it is to help you recognize the difference between your knowledge and your impressions. There's a huge difference between thinking an answer is right because of what you know, and thinking an answer is right because it looks or sounds like it should be right.

Summary: To ensure that your selection is appropriately random, make a predetermined selection from among all answer choices you have not eliminated.

Test-Taking Strategies

This section contains a list of test-taking strategies that you may find helpful as you work through the test. By taking what you know and applying logical thought, you can maximize your chances of answering any question correctly!

It is very important to realize that every question is different and every person is different: no single strategy will work on every question, and no single strategy will work for every person. That's why we've included all of them here, so you can try them out and determine which ones work best for different types of questions and which ones work best for you.

Question Strategies

⊘ Read Carefully

Read the question and the answer choices carefully. Don't miss the question because you misread the terms. You have plenty of time to read each question thoroughly and make sure you understand what is being asked. Yet a happy medium must be attained, so don't waste too much time. You must read carefully and efficiently.

⊘ Contextual Clues

Look for contextual clues. If the question includes a word you are not familiar with, look at the immediate context for some indication of what the word might mean. Contextual clues can often give you all the information you need to decipher the meaning of an unfamiliar word. Even if you can't determine the meaning, you may be able to narrow down the possibilities enough to make a solid guess at the answer to the question.

⊘ Prefixes

If you're having trouble with a word in the question or answer choices, try dissecting it. Take advantage of every clue that the word might include. Prefixes can be a huge help. Usually, they allow you to determine a basic meaning. *Pre-* means before, *post-* means after, *pro-* is positive, *de-* is negative. From prefixes, you can get an idea of the general meaning of the word and try to put it into context.

⊘ Hedge Words

Watch out for critical hedge words, such as *likely, may, can, sometimes, often, almost, mostly, usually, generally, rarely,* and *sometimes.* Question writers insert these hedge phrases to cover every possibility. Often an answer choice will be wrong simply because it leaves no room for exception. Be on guard for answer choices that have definitive words such as *exactly* and *always.*

⊘ Switchback Words

Stay alert for *switchbacks.* These are the words and phrases frequently used to alert you to shifts in thought. The most common switchback words are *but, although,* and *however.* Others include *nevertheless, on the other hand, even though, while, in spite of, despite,* and *regardless of.* Switchback words are important to catch because they can change the direction of the question or an answer choice.

✓ Face Value

When in doubt, use common sense. Accept the situation in the problem at face value. Don't read too much into it. These problems will not require you to make wild assumptions. If you have to go beyond creativity and warp time or space in order to have an answer choice fit the question, then you should move on and consider the other answer choices. These are normal problems rooted in reality. The applicable relationship or explanation may not be readily apparent, but it is there for you to figure out. Use your common sense to interpret anything that isn't clear.

Answer Choice Strategies

✓ Answer Selection

The most thorough way to pick an answer choice is to identify and eliminate wrong answers until only one is left, then confirm it is the correct answer. Sometimes an answer choice may immediately seem right, but be careful. The test writers will usually put more than one reasonable answer choice on each question, so take a second to read all of them and make sure that the other choices are not equally obvious. As long as you have time left, it is better to read every answer choice than to pick the first one that looks right without checking the others.

✓ Answer Choice Families

An answer choice family consists of two (in rare cases, three) answer choices that are very similar in construction and cannot all be true at the same time. If you see two answer choices that are direct opposites or parallels, one of them is usually the correct answer. For instance, if one answer choice says that quantity *x* increases and another either says that quantity *x* decreases (opposite) or says that quantity *y* increases (parallel), then those answer choices would fall into the same family. An answer choice that doesn't match the construction of the answer choice family is more likely to be incorrect. Most questions will not have answer choice families, but when they do appear, you should be prepared to recognize them.

✓ Eliminate Answers

Eliminate answer choices as soon as you realize they are wrong, but make sure you consider all possibilities. If you are eliminating answer choices and realize that the last one you are left with is also wrong, don't panic. Start over and consider each choice again. There may be something you missed the first time that you will realize on the second pass.

✓ Avoid Fact Traps

Don't be distracted by an answer choice that is factually true but doesn't answer the question. You are looking for the choice that answers the question. Stay focused on what the question is asking for so you don't accidentally pick an answer that is true but incorrect. Always go back to the question and make sure the answer choice you've selected actually answers the question and is not merely a true statement.

✓ Extreme Statements

In general, you should avoid answers that put forth extreme actions as standard practice or proclaim controversial ideas as established fact. An answer choice that states the "process should be used in certain situations, if..." is much more likely to be correct than one that states the "process should be discontinued completely." The first is a calm rational statement and doesn't even make a definitive, uncompromising stance, using a hedge word *if* to provide wiggle room, whereas the second choice is far more extreme.

⊘ Benchmark

As you read through the answer choices and you come across one that seems to answer the question well, mentally select that answer choice. This is not your final answer, but it's the one that will help you evaluate the other answer choices. The one that you selected is your benchmark or standard for judging each of the other answer choices. Every other answer choice must be compared to your benchmark. That choice is correct until proven otherwise by another answer choice beating it. If you find a better answer, then that one becomes your new benchmark. Once you've decided that no other choice answers the question as well as your benchmark, you have your final answer.

⊘ Predict the Answer

Before you even start looking at the answer choices, it is often best to try to predict the answer. When you come up with the answer on your own, it is easier to avoid distractions and traps because you will know exactly what to look for. The right answer choice is unlikely to be word-for-word what you came up with, but it should be a close match. Even if you are confident that you have the right answer, you should still take the time to read each option before moving on.

General Strategies

⊘ Tough Questions

If you are stumped on a problem or it appears too hard or too difficult, don't waste time. Move on! Remember though, if you can quickly check for obviously incorrect answer choices, your chances of guessing correctly are greatly improved. Before you completely give up, at least try to knock out a couple of possible answers. Eliminate what you can and then guess at the remaining answer choices before moving on.

⊘ Check Your Work

Since you will probably not know every term listed and the answer to every question, it is important that you get credit for the ones that you do know. Don't miss any questions through careless mistakes. If at all possible, try to take a second to look back over your answer selection and make sure you've selected the correct answer choice and haven't made a costly careless mistake (such as marking an answer choice that you didn't mean to mark). This quick double check should more than pay for itself in caught mistakes for the time it costs.

⊘ Pace Yourself

It's easy to be overwhelmed when you're looking at a page full of questions; your mind is confused and full of random thoughts, and the clock is ticking down faster than you would like. Calm down and maintain the pace that you have set for yourself. Especially as you get down to the last few minutes of the test, don't let the small numbers on the clock make you panic. As long as you are on track by monitoring your pace, you are guaranteed to have time for each question.

⊘ Don't Rush

It is very easy to make errors when you are in a hurry. Maintaining a fast pace in answering questions is pointless if it makes you miss questions that you would have gotten right otherwise. Test writers like to include distracting information and wrong answers that seem right. Taking a little extra time to avoid careless mistakes can make all the difference in your test score. Find a pace that allows you to be confident in the answers that you select.

☑ Keep Moving

Panicking will not help you pass the test, so do your best to stay calm and keep moving. Taking deep breaths and going through the answer elimination steps you practiced can help to break through a stress barrier and keep your pace.

Final Notes

The combination of a solid foundation of content knowledge and the confidence that comes from practicing your plan for applying that knowledge is the key to maximizing your performance on test day. As your foundation of content knowledge is built up and strengthened, you'll find that the strategies included in this chapter become more and more effective in helping you quickly sift through the distractions and traps of the test to isolate the correct answer.

Now that you're preparing to move forward into the test content chapters of this book, be sure to keep your goal in mind. As you read, think about how you will be able to apply this information on the test. If you've already seen sample questions for the test and you have an idea of the question format and style, try to come up with questions of your own that you can answer based on what you're reading. This will give you valuable practice applying your knowledge in the same ways you can expect to on test day.

Good luck and good studying!

Writing Ability

Clarity

Clarity simply means *clearness*, and it's another very important aspect of communication, especially written communication. It's vitally important for a peace officer to write in such a way that the meaning of the written communication is crystal clear; there should be no doubt as to the exact meaning. This section will cover the basics of grammar as it relates to clear written communication.

Subjects and Predicates

Subjects

The **subject** of a sentence names who or what the sentence is about. The subject may be directly stated in a sentence, or the subject may be the implied *you*. The **complete subject** includes the simple subject and all of its modifiers. To find the complete subject, ask *Who* or *What* and insert the verb to complete the question. The answer, including any modifiers (adjectives, prepositional phrases, etc.), is the complete subject. To find the **simple subject**, remove all of the modifiers in the complete subject. Being able to locate the subject of a sentence helps with many problems, such as those involving sentence fragments and subject-verb agreement.

Examples:

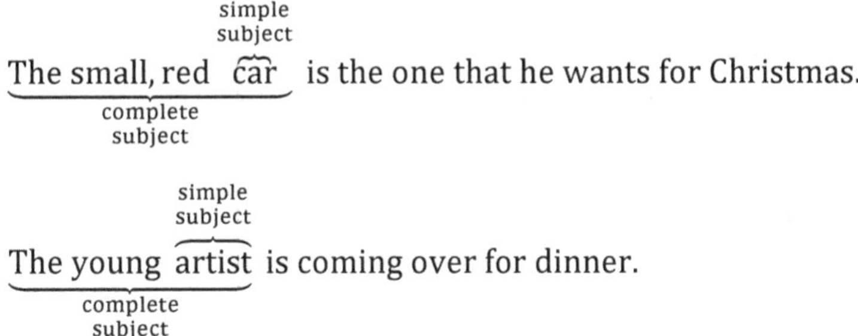

Review Video: Subjects in English
Visit mometrix.com/academy and enter code: 444771

In **imperative** sentences, the verb's subject is understood (e.g., [You] Run to the store), but is not actually present in the sentence. Normally, the subject comes before the verb. However, the subject comes after the verb in sentences that begin with *There are* or *There was.*

Direct:

John knows the way to the park.	Who knows the way to the park?	John
The cookies need ten more minutes.	What needs ten minutes?	The cookies
By five o'clock, Bill will need to leave.	Who needs to leave?	Bill
There are five letters on the table for him.	What is on the table?	Five letters
There were coffee and doughnuts in the house.	What was in the house?	Coffee and doughnuts

Implied:

Go to the post office for me.	Who is going to the post office?	You
Come and sit with me, please?	Who needs to come and sit?	You

PREDICATES

In a sentence, you always have a predicate and a subject. The subject tells who or what the sentence is about, and the **predicate** explains or describes the subject. The predicate includes the verb or verb phrase and any direct or indirect objects of the verb, as well as any words or phrases modifying these.

Think about the sentence *He sings.* In this sentence, we have a subject (He) and a predicate (sings). This is all that is needed for a sentence to be complete. Most sentences contain more information, but if this is all the information that you are given, then you have a complete sentence.

Now, let's look at another sentence: *John and Jane sing on Tuesday nights at the dance hall.*

subject: John and Jane | predicate: sing on Tuesday nights at the dance hall.

Review Video: Complete Predicate
Visit mometrix.com/academy and enter code: 293942

SUBJECT-VERB AGREEMENT

Verbs must **agree** with their subjects in number and in person. To agree in number, singular subjects need singular verbs and plural subjects need plural verbs. A **singular** noun refers to **one** person, place, or thing. A **plural** noun refers to **more than one** person, place, or thing. To agree in person, the correct verb form must be chosen to match the first, second, or third person subject. The present tense ending *-s* or *-es* is used on a verb if its subject is third person singular; otherwise, the verb's ending is not modified.

Review Video: Subject-Verb Agreement
Visit mometrix.com/academy and enter code: 479190

Number Agreement Examples:

Single Subject and Verb: Dan [singular subject] calls [singular verb] home.

Dan is one person. So, the singular verb *calls* is needed.

Plural Subject and Verb: Dan and Bob [plural subject] call [plural verb] home.

More than one person needs the plural verb *call.*

Person Agreement Examples:

First Person: I *am* walking.

Second Person: You *are* walking.

Third Person: He *is* walking.

Complications with Subject-Verb Agreement

Words Between Subject and Verb

Words that come between the simple subject and the verb have no bearing on subject-verb agreement.

Examples:

The joy [singular subject] of my life returns [singular verb] home tonight.

The phrase *of my life* does not influence the verb *returns.*

The question [singular subject] that still remains unanswered is [singular verb] "Who are you?"

Don't let the phrase "*that still remains*..." trouble you. The subject *question* goes with *is.*

Compound Subjects

A compound subject is formed when two or more nouns joined by *and, or,* or *nor* jointly act as the subject of the sentence.

Joined by And

When a compound subject is joined by *and,* it is treated as a plural subject and requires a plural verb.

Examples:

You and Jon [plural subject] are [plural verb] invited to come to my house.

The pencil and paper [plural subject] belong [plural verb] to me.

Joined by Or/Nor

For a compound subject joined by *or* or *nor*, the verb must agree in number with the part of the subject that is closest to the verb (italicized in the examples below).

Examples:

subject — verb
Today or tomorrow is the day.

subject — verb
Stan or Phil wants to read the book.

subject — verb
Neither the pen nor the book is on the desk.

subject — verb
Either the blanket or pillows arrive this afternoon.

Indefinite Pronouns as Subject

An indefinite pronoun is a pronoun that does not refer to a specific noun. Some indefinite pronouns function as only singular, some function as only plural, and some can function as either singular or plural depending on how they are used.

Always Singular

Pronouns such as *each*, *either*, *everybody*, *anybody*, *somebody*, and *nobody* are always singular.

Examples:

singular subject — singular verb
Each of the runners has a different bib number.

singular verb — singular subject
Is either of you ready for the game?

Note: The words *each* and *either* can also be used as adjectives (e.g., *each* person is unique). When one of these adjectives modifies the subject of a sentence, it is always a singular subject.

singular subject — singular verb
Everybody grows a day older every day.

singular subject — singular verb
Anybody is welcome to bring a tent.

Always Plural

Pronouns such as *both*, *several*, and *many* are always plural.

Examples:

Both (plural subject) of the siblings were (plural verb) too tired to argue.

Many (plural subject) have tried (plural verb), but none have succeeded.

Depend on Context

Pronouns such as *some*, *any*, *all*, *none*, *more*, and *most* can be either singular or plural depending on what they are representing in the context of the sentence.

Examples:

All (singular subject) of my dog's food was (singular verb) still there in his bowl.

By the end of the night, all (plural subject) of my guests were (plural verb) already excited about coming to my next party.

Other Cases Involving Plural or Irregular Form

Some nouns are **singular in meaning but plural in form**: news, mathematics, physics, and economics.

The *news is* coming on now.

Mathematics is my favorite class.

Some nouns are plural in form and meaning, and have **no singular equivalent**: scissors and pants.

Do these *pants come* with a shirt?

The *scissors are* for my project.

Mathematical operations are **irregular** in their construction, but are normally considered to be **singular in meaning**.

One plus one is two.

Three times three is nine.

Note: Look to your **dictionary** for help when you aren't sure whether a noun with a plural form has a singular or plural meaning.

Complements

A complement is a noun, pronoun, or adjective that is used to give more information about the subject or object in the sentence.

Direct Objects

A direct object is a noun or pronoun that tells who or what **receives** the action of the verb. A sentence will only include a direct object if the verb is a transitive verb. If the verb is an intransitive verb or a linking verb, there will be no direct object. When you are looking for a direct object, find the verb and ask *who* or *what.*

Examples:

> I took *the blanket.*
>
> Jane read *books.*

Indirect Objects

An indirect object is a noun or pronoun that indicates what or whom the action had an **influence** on. If there is an indirect object in a sentence, then there will also be a direct object. When you are looking for the indirect object, find the verb and ask *to/for whom or what.*

Examples:

> We taught the old dog (indirect object) a new trick (direct object).
>
> I gave them (indirect object) a math lesson (direct object).

Review Video: Direct and Indirect Objects
Visit mometrix.com/academy and enter code: 817385

Predicate Nominatives and Predicate Adjectives

As we looked at previously, verbs may be classified as either action verbs or linking verbs. A linking verb is so named because it links the subject to words in the predicate that describe or define the subject. These words are called predicate nominatives (if nouns or pronouns) or predicate adjectives (if adjectives).

Examples:

> My father (subject) is a lawyer (predicate nominative).
>
> Your mother (subject) is patient (predicate adjective).

Pronoun Usage

The **antecedent** is the noun that has been replaced by a pronoun. A pronoun and its antecedent **agree** when they have the same number (singular or plural) and gender (male, female, or neutral).

Examples:

antecedent pronoun

Singular agreement: John came into town, and he played for us.

antecedent pronoun

Plural agreement: John and Rick came into town, and they played for us.

To determine which is the correct pronoun to use in a compound subject or object, try each pronoun **alone** in place of the compound in the sentence. Your knowledge of pronouns will tell you which one is correct.

Example:

Bob and (I, me) will be going.

Test: (1) *I will be going* or (2) *Me will be going*. The second choice cannot be correct because *me* cannot be used as the subject of a sentence. Instead, *me* is used as an object.

Answer: Bob and I will be going.

When a pronoun is used with a noun immediately following (as in "we boys"), try the sentence **without the added noun**.

Example:

(We/Us) boys played football last year.

Test: (1) *We played football last ye*ar or (2) *Us played football last year*. Again, the second choice cannot be correct because *us* cannot be used as a subject of a sentence. Instead, *us* is used as an object.

Answer: We boys played football last year.

Review Video: Pronoun Usage
Visit mometrix.com/academy and enter code: 666500

Review Video: Pronoun-Antecedent Agreement
Visit mometrix.com/academy and enter code: 919704

A pronoun should point clearly to the **antecedent**. Here is how a pronoun reference can be unhelpful if it is puzzling or not directly stated.

antecedent pronoun

Unhelpful: Ron and Jim went to the store, and he bought soda.

Who bought soda? Ron or Jim?

antecedent pronoun

Helpful: Jim went to the store, and he bought soda.

The sentence is clear. Jim bought the soda.

Some pronouns change their form by their placement in a sentence. A pronoun that is a **subject** in a sentence comes in the **subjective case**. Pronouns that serve as **objects** appear in the **objective case**. Finally, the pronouns that are used as **possessives** appear in the **possessive case**.

Examples:

> **Subjective case**: *He* is coming to the show.
>
> The pronoun *He* is the subject of the sentence.
>
> **Objective case**: Josh drove *him* to the airport.
>
> The pronoun *him* is the object of the sentence.
>
> **Possessive case**: The flowers are *mine*.
>
> The pronoun *mine* shows ownership of the flowers.

The word *who* is a subjective-case pronoun that can be used as a **subject**. The word *whom* is an objective-case pronoun that can be used as an **object**. The words *who* and *whom* are common in subordinate clauses or in questions.

Examples:

> He knows who (subject) wants (verb) to come.
>
> He knows the man whom (object) we want (verb) at the party.

CLAUSES

A clause is a group of words that contains both a subject and a predicate (verb). There are two types of clauses: independent and dependent. An **independent clause** contains a complete thought, while a **dependent (or subordinate) clause** does not. A dependent clause includes a subject and a verb, and may also contain objects or complements, but it cannot stand as a complete thought without being joined to an independent clause. Dependent clauses function within sentences as adjectives, adverbs, or nouns.

Example:

> I am running (independent clause) because I want to stay in shape. (dependent clause)

The clause *I am running* is an independent clause: it has a subject and a verb, and it gives a complete thought. The clause *because I want to stay in shape* is a dependent clause: it has a subject and a verb, but it does not express a complete thought. It adds detail to the independent clause to which it is attached.

Review Video: Clauses
Visit mometrix.com/academy and enter code: 940170

Review Video: Independent and Dependent Clauses
Visit mometrix.com/academy and enter code: 556903

Types of Dependent Clauses

Adjective Clauses

An **adjective clause** is a dependent clause that modifies a noun or a pronoun. Adjective clauses begin with a relative pronoun (*who, whose, whom, which,* and *that*) or a relative adverb (*where, when,* and *why*).

Also, adjective clauses usually come immediately after the noun that the clause needs to explain or rename. This is done to ensure that it is clear which noun or pronoun the clause is modifying.

Examples:

I learned the reason (independent clause) why I won the award. (adjective clause)

This is the place (independent clause) where I started my first job. (adjective clause)

An adjective clause can be an essential or nonessential clause. An essential clause is very important to the sentence. **Essential clauses** explain or define a person or thing. **Nonessential clauses** give more information about a person or thing but are not necessary to define them. Nonessential clauses are set off with commas while essential clauses are not.

Examples:

A person who works hard at first (essential clause) can often rest later in life.

Neil Armstrong, who walked on the moon, (nonessential clause) is my hero.

Review Video: Adjective Clauses and Phrases
Visit mometrix.com/academy and enter code: 520888

Adverb Clauses

An **adverb clause** is a dependent clause that modifies a verb, adjective, or adverb. In sentences with multiple dependent clauses, adverb clauses are usually placed immediately before or after the independent clause. An adverb clause is introduced with words such as *after, although, as, before, because, if, since, so, unless, when, where,* and *while.*

Examples:

When you walked outside, (adverb clause) I called the manager.

I will go with you unless you want to stay. (adverb clause)

Noun Clauses

A **noun clause** is a dependent clause that can be used as a subject, object, or complement. Noun clauses begin with words such as *how, that, what, whether, which, who,* and *why*. These words can also come with an adjective clause. Unless the noun clause is being used as the subject of the sentence, it should come after the verb of the independent clause.

Examples:

noun clause

The real mystery is how you avoided serious injury.

noun clause

What you learn from each other depends on your honesty with others.

SUBORDINATION

When two related ideas are not of equal importance, the ideal way to combine them is to make the more important idea an independent clause and the less important idea a dependent or subordinate clause. This is called **subordination**.

Example:

Separate ideas: The team had a perfect regular season. The team lost the championship.

Subordinated: Despite having a perfect regular season, *the team lost the championship.*

PHRASES

A phrase is a group of words that functions as a single part of speech, usually a noun, adjective, or adverb. A **phrase** is not a complete thought and does not contain a subject and predicate, but it adds detail or explanation to a sentence, or renames something within the sentence.

PREPOSITIONAL PHRASES

One of the most common types of phrases is the prepositional phrase. A **prepositional phrase** begins with a preposition and ends with a noun or pronoun that is the object of the preposition. Normally, the prepositional phrase functions as an **adjective** or an **adverb** within the sentence.

Examples:

prepositional phrase

The picnic is on the blanket.

prepositional phrase

I am sick with a fever today.

prepositional phrase

Among the many flowers, John found a four-leaf clover.

Verbal Phrases

A **verbal** is a word or phrase that is formed from a verb but does not function as a verb. Depending on its particular form, it may be used as a noun, adjective, or adverb. A verbal does **not** replace a verb in a sentence.

Examples:

Correct: Walk (verb) a mile daily.

This is a complete sentence with the implied subject *you*.

Incorrect: To walk (verbal) a mile.

This is not a sentence since there is no functional verb.

There are three types of verbal: **participles**, **gerunds**, and **infinitives**. Each type of verbal has a corresponding **phrase** that consists of the verbal itself along with any complements or modifiers.

Participles

A **participle** is a type of verbal that always functions as an adjective. The present participle always ends with *-ing*. Past participles end with *-d, -ed, -n,* or *-t.* Participles are combined with helping verbs to form certain verb tenses, but a participle by itself cannot function as a verb.

Examples: dance (verb) | dancing (present participle) | danced (past participle)

Participial phrases most often come right before or right after the noun or pronoun that they modify.

Examples:

Shipwrecked on an island, (participial phrase) the boys started to fish for food.

Having been seated for five hours, (participial phrase) we got out of the car to stretch our legs.

Praised for their work, (participial phrase) the group accepted the first-place trophy.

Gerunds

A **gerund** is a type of verbal that always functions as a **noun**. Like present participles, gerunds always end with *-ing*, but they can be easily distinguished from participles by the part of speech they represent (participles always function as adjectives). Since a gerund or gerund phrase always functions as a noun, it can be used as the subject of a sentence, the predicate nominative, or the object of a verb or preposition.

Examples:

gerund

We want to be known for teaching the poor.

object of preposition

gerund

Coaching this team is the best job of my life.

subject

gerund

We like practicing our songs in the basement.

object of verb

INFINITIVES

An **infinitive** is a type of verbal that can function as a noun, an adjective, or an adverb. An infinitive is made of the word *to* and the basic form of the verb. As with all other types of verbal phrases, an infinitive phrase includes the verbal itself and all of its complements or modifiers.

Examples:

infinitive

To join the team is my goal in life.

noun

infinitive

The animals have enough food to eat for the night.

adjective

infinitive

People lift weights to exercise their muscles.

adverb

Review Video: Verbals
Visit mometrix.com/academy and enter code: 915480

APPOSITIVE PHRASES

An **appositive** is a word or phrase that is used to explain or rename nouns or pronouns. Noun phrases, gerund phrases, and infinitive phrases can all be used as appositives.

Examples:

appositive

Terriers, hunters at heart, have been dressed up to look like lap dogs.

The noun phrase *hunters at heart* renames the noun *terriers.*

appositive

His plan, to save and invest his money, was proven as a safe approach.

The infinitive phrase explains what the plan is.

Appositive phrases can be **essential** or **nonessential**. An appositive phrase is essential if the person, place, or thing being described or renamed is too general for its meaning to be understood without the appositive.

Examples:

> essential
>
> Two of America's Founding Fathers, George Washington and Thomas Jefferson, served as presidents.

> nonessential
>
> George Washington and Thomas Jefferson, two Founding Fathers, served as presidents.

Absolute Phrases

An absolute phrase is a phrase that consists of **a noun followed by a participle**. An absolute phrase provides **context** to what is being described in the sentence, but it does not modify or explain any particular word; it is essentially independent.

Examples:

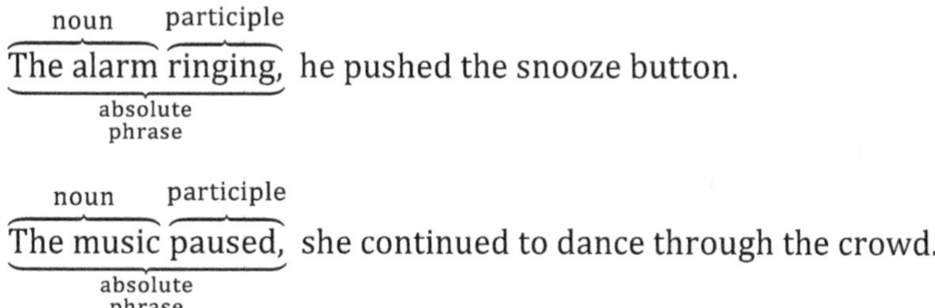
noun
participle
The alarm ringing, he pushed the snooze button.
absolute phrase
noun
participle
The music paused, she continued to dance through the crowd.
absolute phrase

Parallelism

When multiple items or ideas are presented in a sentence in series, such as in a list, the items or ideas must be stated in grammatically equivalent ways. For example, if two ideas are listed in parallel and the first is stated in gerund form, the second cannot be stated in infinitive form. (e.g., *I enjoy reading and to study.* [incorrect]) An infinitive and a gerund are not grammatically equivalent. Instead, you should write *I enjoy reading and studying* OR *I like to read and to study*. In lists of more than two, all items must be parallel.

Example:

> **Incorrect**: He stopped at the office, grocery store, and the pharmacy before heading home.
>
> The first and third items in the list of places include the article *the*, so the second item needs it as well.
>
> **Correct**: He stopped at the office, *the* grocery store, and the pharmacy before heading home.

Example:

Incorrect: While vacationing in Europe, she went biking, skiing, and climbed mountains.

The first and second items in the list are gerunds, so the third item must be as well.

Correct: While vacationing in Europe, she went biking, skiing, and *mountain climbing*.

Review Video: Parallel Sentence Construction
Visit mometrix.com/academy and enter code: 831988

Sentence Purpose

There are four types of sentences: declarative, imperative, interrogative, and exclamatory.

A **declarative** sentence states a fact and ends with a period.

The football game starts at seven o'clock.

An **imperative** sentence tells someone to do something and generally ends with a period. An urgent command might end with an exclamation point instead.

Don't forget to buy your ticket.

An **interrogative** sentence asks a question and ends with a question mark.

Are you going to the game on Friday?

An **exclamatory** sentence shows strong emotion and ends with an exclamation point.

I can't believe we won the game!

Sentence Structure

Sentences are classified by structure based on the type and number of clauses present. The four classifications of sentence structure are the following:

Simple: A simple sentence has one independent clause with no dependent clauses. A simple sentence may have **compound elements** (i.e., compound subject or verb).

Examples:

single subject | single verb

Judy watered the lawn.

compound subject | single verb

Judy and Alan watered the lawn.

single subject | compound verb | compound verb

Judy watered the lawn and pulled weeds.

compound subject | compound verb | compound verb

Judy and Alan watered the lawn and pulled weeds.

Compound: A compound sentence has two or more independent clauses with no dependent clauses. Usually, the independent clauses are joined with a comma and a coordinating conjunction or with a semicolon.

Examples:

independent clause | independent clause

The time has come, and we are ready.

independent clause | independent clause

I woke up at dawn; the sun was just coming up.

Complex: A complex sentence has one independent clause and at least one dependent clause.

Examples:

dependent clause | independent clause

Although he had the flu, Harry went to work.

independent clause | dependent clause

Marcia got married, after she finished college.

Compound-Complex: A compound-complex sentence has at least two independent clauses and at least one dependent clause.

Examples:

independent clause | dependent clause | independent clause

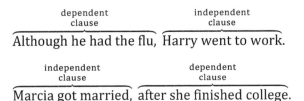

John is my friend who went to India, and he brought back souvenirs.

independent clause | independent clause | dependent clause

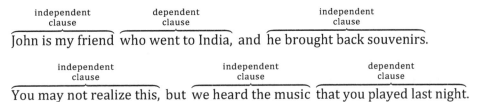

You may not realize this, but we heard the music that you played last night.

Review Video: Sentence Structure
Visit mometrix.com/academy and enter code: 700478

Sentence variety is important to consider when writing an essay or speech. A variety of sentence lengths and types creates rhythm, makes a passage more engaging, and gives writers an opportunity to demonstrate their writing style. Writing that uses the same length or type of sentence without variation can be boring or difficult to read. To evaluate a passage for effective sentence variety, it is helpful to note whether the passage contains diverse sentence structures and lengths. It is also important to pay attention to the way each sentence starts and avoid beginning with the same words or phrases.

Sentence Fragments

Recall that a group of words must contain at least one **independent clause** in order to be considered a sentence. If it doesn't contain even one independent clause, it is called a **sentence fragment**.

The appropriate process for **repairing** a sentence fragment depends on what type of fragment it is. If the fragment is a dependent clause, it can sometimes be as simple as removing a subordinating word (e.g., when, because, if) from the beginning of the fragment. Alternatively, a dependent clause can be incorporated into a closely related neighboring sentence. If the fragment is missing some required part, like a subject or a verb, the fix might be as simple as adding the missing part.

Examples:

> **Fragment**: Because he wanted to sail the Mediterranean.
>
> **Removed subordinating word**: He wanted to sail the Mediterranean.
>
> **Combined with another sentence**: Because he wanted to sail the Mediterranean, he booked a Greek island cruise.

Run-on Sentences

Run-on sentences consist of multiple independent clauses that have not been joined together properly. Run-on sentences can be corrected in several different ways:

Join clauses properly: This can be done with a comma and coordinating conjunction, with a semicolon, or with a colon or dash if the second clause is explaining something in the first.

Example:

> **Incorrect**: I went on the trip, we visited lots of castles.
>
> **Corrected**: I went on the trip, and we visited lots of castles.

Split into separate sentences: This correction is most effective when the independent clauses are very long or when they are not closely related.

Example:

> **Incorrect**: The drive to New York takes ten hours, my uncle lives in Boston.
>
> **Corrected**: The drive to New York takes ten hours. My uncle lives in Boston.

Make one clause dependent: This is the easiest way to make the sentence correct and more interesting at the same time. It's often as simple as adding a subordinating word between the two clauses or before the first clause.

Example:

Incorrect: I finally made it to the store and I bought some eggs.

Corrected: When I finally made it to the store, I bought some eggs.

Reduce to one clause with a compound verb: If both clauses have the same subject, remove the subject from the second clause, and you now have just one clause with a compound verb.

Example:

Incorrect: The drive to New York takes ten hours, it makes me very tired.

Corrected: The drive to New York takes ten hours and makes me very tired.

Note: While these are the simplest ways to correct a run-on sentence, often the best way is to completely reorganize the thoughts in the sentence and rewrite it.

Review Video: Fragments and Run-on Sentences
Visit mometrix.com/academy and enter code: 541989

Dangling and Misplaced Modifiers

Dangling Modifiers

A dangling modifier is a dependent clause or verbal phrase that does not have a clear logical connection to a word in the sentence.

Example:

dangling modifier

Incorrect: Reading each magazine article, the stories caught my attention.

The word *stories* cannot be modified by *Reading each magazine article*. People can read, but stories cannot read. Therefore, the subject of the sentence must be a person.

gerund phrase

Corrected: Reading each magazine article, I was entertained by the stories.

Example:

dangling modifier

Incorrect: Ever since childhood, my grandparents have visited me for Christmas.

The speaker in this sentence can't have been visited by her grandparents when *they* were children, since she wouldn't have been born yet. Either the modifier should be clarified or the sentence should be rearranged to specify whose childhood is being referenced.

dependent clause

Clarified: Ever since I was a child, my grandparents have visited for Christmas.

adverb phrase

Rearranged: Ever since childhood, I have enjoyed my grandparents visiting for Christmas.

MISPLACED MODIFIERS

Because modifiers are grammatically versatile, they can be put in many different places within the structure of a sentence. The danger of this versatility is that a modifier can accidentally be placed where it is modifying the wrong word or where it is not clear which word it is modifying.

Example:

> **Incorrect**: She read the book to a crowd that was filled with beautiful pictures. (modifier: "that was filled with beautiful pictures")
>
> The book was filled with beautiful pictures, not the crowd.
>
> **Corrected**: She read the book that was filled with beautiful pictures to a crowd. (modifier: "that was filled with beautiful pictures")

Example:

> **Ambiguous**: Derek saw a bus nearly hit a man on his way to work. (modifier: "on his way to work")
>
> Was Derek on his way to work or was the other man?
>
> **Derek**: On his way to work, Derek saw a bus nearly hit a man. (modifier: "On his way to work")
>
> **The other man**: Derek saw a bus nearly hit a man who was on his way to work. (modifier: "who was on his way to work")

SPLIT INFINITIVES

A split infinitive occurs when a modifying word comes between the word *to* and the verb that pairs with *to*.

> Example: To *clearly* explain vs. *To explain* clearly | To *softly* sing vs. *To sing* softly

Though considered improper by some, split infinitives may provide better clarity and simplicity in some cases than the alternatives. As such, avoiding them should not be considered a universal rule.

DOUBLE NEGATIVES

Standard English allows **two negatives** only when a **positive** meaning is intended. (e.g., The team was *not displeased* with their performance.) Double negatives to emphasize negation are not used in standard English.

Negative modifiers (e.g., never, no, and not) should not be paired with other negative modifiers or negative words (e.g., none, nobody, nothing, or neither). The modifiers *hardly, barely,* and *scarcely* are also considered negatives in standard English, so they should not be used with other negatives.

Word Confusion

Which, That, and Who

The words *which, that,* and *who* can act as **relative pronouns** to help clarify or describe a noun.

Which is used for things only.

Example: Andrew's car, *which is old and rusty,* broke down last week.

That is used for people or things. *That* is usually informal when used to describe people.

Example: Is this the only book *that Louis L'Amour wrote?*

Example: Is Louis L'Amour the author *that wrote Western novels?*

Who is used for people or for animals that have an identity or personality.

Example: Mozart was the composer *who wrote those operas.*

Example: John's dog, *who is called Max,* is large and fierce.

Homophones

Homophones are words that sound alike (or similar) but have different **spellings** and **definitions.** A homophone is a type of **homonym**, which is a pair or group of words that are pronounced or spelled the same, but do not mean the same thing.

To, Too, and Two

To can be an adverb or a preposition for showing direction, purpose, and relationship. See your dictionary for the many other ways to use *to* in a sentence.

Examples: I went to the store. | I want to go with you.

Too is an adverb that means *also, as well, very,* or *in excess.*

Examples: I can walk a mile too. | You have eaten too much.

Two is a number.

Example: You have two minutes left.

There, Their, and They're

There can be an adjective, adverb, or pronoun. Often, *there* is used to show a place or to start a sentence.

Examples: I went there yesterday. | There is something in his pocket.

Their is a pronoun that is used to show ownership.

Examples: He is their father. | This is their fourth apology this week.

They're is a contraction of *they are.*

Example: Did you know that they're in town?

Knew and New

Knew is the past tense of *know*.

Example: I knew the answer.

New is an adjective that means something is current, has not been used, or is modern.

Example: This is my new phone.

Then and Than

Then is an adverb that indicates sequence or order:

Example: I'm going to run to the library and then come home.

Than is special-purpose word used only for comparisons:

Example: Susie likes chips more than candy.

Its and It's

Its is a pronoun that shows ownership.

Example: The guitar is in its case.

It's is a contraction of *it is*.

Example: It's an honor and a privilege to meet you.

Note: The *h* in honor is silent, so *honor* starts with the vowel sound *o*, which must have the article *an*.

Your and You're

Your is a pronoun that shows ownership.

Example: This is your moment to shine.

You're is a contraction of *you are*.

Example: Yes, you're correct.

Saw and Seen

Saw is the past-tense form of *see*.

Example: I saw a turtle on my walk this morning.

Seen is the past participle of *see*.

Example: I have seen this movie before.

Affect and Effect

There are two main reasons that *affect* and *effect* are so often confused: 1) both words can be used as either a noun or a verb, and 2) unlike most homophones, their usage and meanings are closely related to each other. Here is a quick rundown of the four usage options:

Affect (n): feeling, emotion, or mood that is displayed

Example: The patient had a flat *affect*. (i.e., his face showed little or no emotion)

Affect (v): to alter, to change, to influence

Example: The sunshine *affects* the plant's growth.

Effect (n): a result, a consequence

Example: What *effect* will this weather have on our schedule?

Effect (v): to bring about, to cause to be

Example: These new rules will *effect* order in the office.

The noun form of *affect* is rarely used outside of technical medical descriptions, so if a noun form is needed on the test, you can safely select *effect*. The verb form of *effect* is not as rare as the noun form of *affect*, but it's still not all that likely to show up on your test. If you need a verb and you can't decide which to use based on the definitions, choosing *affect* is your best bet.

Homographs

Homographs are words that share the same spelling, but have different meanings and sometimes different pronunciations. To figure out which meaning is being used, you should be looking for context clues. The context clues give hints to the meaning of the word. For example, the word *spot* has many meanings. It can mean "a place" or "a stain or blot." In the sentence "After my lunch, I saw a spot on my shirt," the word *spot* means "a stain or blot." The context clues of "After my lunch" and "on my shirt" guide you to this decision. A homograph is another type of homonym.

Bank

(noun): an establishment where money is held for savings or lending

(verb): to collect or pile up

Content

(noun): the topics that will be addressed within a book

(adjective): pleased or satisfied

(verb): to make someone pleased or satisfied

Fine

(noun): an amount of money that acts a penalty for an offense

(adjective): very small or thin

(adverb): in an acceptable way

(verb): to make someone pay money as a punishment

Incense

(noun): a material that is burned in religious settings and makes a pleasant aroma

(verb): to frustrate or anger

Lead

(noun): the first or highest position

(noun): a heavy metallic element

(verb): to direct a person or group of followers

(adjective): containing lead

Object

(noun): a lifeless item that can be held and observed

(verb): to disagree

Produce

(noun): fruits and vegetables

(verb): to make or create something

Refuse

(noun): garbage or debris that has been thrown away

(verb): to not allow

Subject

(noun): an area of study

(verb): to force or subdue

Tear

(noun): a fluid secreted by the eyes

(verb): to separate or pull apart

Commonly Misused Words and Phrases

A Lot

The phrase *a lot* should always be written as two words; never as *alot.*

Correct: That's a lot of chocolate!

Incorrect: He does that alot.

Can

The word *can* is used to describe things that are possible occurrences; the word *may* is used to described things that are allowed to happen.

Correct: May I have another piece of pie?

Correct: I can lift three of these bags of mulch at a time.

Incorrect: Mom said we can stay up thirty minutes later tonight.

Could Have

The phrase *could of* is often incorrectly substituted for the phrase *could have*. Similarly, *could of*, *may of*, and *might of* are sometimes used in place of the correct phrases *could have*, *may have*, and *might have*.

Correct: If I had known, I would have helped out.

Incorrect: Well, that could of gone much worse than it did.

Myself

The word *myself* is a reflexive pronoun, often incorrectly used in place of *I* or *me*.

Correct: He let me do it myself.

Incorrect: The job was given to Dave and myself.

Off

The phrase *off of* is a redundant expression that should be avoided. In most cases, it can be corrected simply by removing *of*.

Correct: My dog chased the squirrel off its perch on the fence.

Incorrect: He finally moved his plate off of the table.

Supposed To

The phrase *suppose to* is sometimes used incorrectly in place of the phrase *supposed to*.

Correct: I was supposed to go to the store this afternoon.

Incorrect: When are we suppose to get our grades?

Try To

The phrase *try and* is often used in informal writing and conversation to replace the correct phrase *try to*.

Correct: It's a good policy to try to satisfy every customer who walks in the door.

Incorrect: Don't try and do too much.

Spelling

Peace officers must have very good spelling skills. Writing reports is an important part of the job, and there are other aspects of the job that also require written communication. Without the ability to spell properly an officer would not be able to write a good report. At best, bad spelling looks unprofessional; at worst, it can lead to misunderstandings, which could cause even bigger problems.

General Spelling Rules

Words Ending with a Consonant

Usually, the final consonant is **doubled** on a word before adding a suffix. This is the rule for single syllable words, words ending with one consonant, and multi-syllable words with the last syllable accented. The following are examples:

- *beg* becomes *begging* (single syllable)
- *shop* becomes *shopped* (single syllable)
- *add* becomes *adding* (already ends in double consonant, do not add another *d*)
- *deter* becomes *deterring* (multi-syllable, accent on last syllable)
- *regret* becomes *regrettable* (multi-syllable, accent on last syllable)
- *compost* becomes *composting* (do not add another *t* because the accent is on the first syllable)

Words Ending with Y or C

The general rule for words ending in *y* is to keep the *y* when adding a suffix if the **y is preceded by a vowel**. If the word **ends in a consonant and y** the *y* is changed to an *i* before the suffix is added (unless the suffix itself begins with *i*). The following are examples:

- *pay* becomes *paying* (keep the *y*)
- *bully* becomes *bullied* (change to *i*)
- *bully* becomes *bullying* (keep the *y* because the suffix is *-ing*)

If a word ends with *c* and the suffix begins with an *e, i,* or *y*, the letter *k* is usually added to the end of the word. The following are examples:

- panic becomes panicky
- mimic becomes mimicking

Words Containing IE or EI, and/or Ending with E

Most words are spelled with an *i* before *e*, except when they follow the letter *c*, **or** sound like *a*. For example, the following words are spelled correctly according to these rules:

- piece, friend, believe (*i* before *e*)
- receive, ceiling, conceited (except after *c*)
- weight, neighborhood, veil (sounds like *a*)

To add a suffix to words ending with the letter *e*, first determine if the *e* is silent. If it is, the *e* will be kept if the added suffix begins with a consonant. If the suffix begins with a vowel, the *e* is dropped. The following are examples:

- *age* becomes *ageless* (keep the *e*)
- *age* becomes *aging* (drop the *e*)

An exception to this rule occurs when the word ends in *ce* or *ge* and the suffix *able* or *ous* is added; these words will retain the letter *e*. The following are examples:

- courage becomes courageous
- notice becomes noticeable

Words Ending with ise or ize

A small number of words end with *ise*. Most of the words in the English language with the same sound end in *ize*. The following are examples:

- advertise, advise, arise, chastise, circumcise, and comprise
- compromise, demise, despise, devise, disguise, enterprise, excise, and exercise
- franchise, improvise, incise, merchandise, premise, reprise, and revise
- supervise, surmise, surprise, and televise

Words that end with *ize* include the following:

- accessorize, agonize, authorize, and brutalize
- capitalize, caramelize, categorize, civilize, and demonize
- downsize, empathize, euthanize, idolize, and immunize
- legalize, metabolize, mobilize, organize, and ostracize
- plagiarize, privatize, utilize, and visualize

(Note that some words may technically be spelled with *ise*, especially in British English, but it is more common to use *ize*. Examples include *symbolize/symbolise* and *baptize/baptise*.)

Words Ending with ceed, sede, or cede

There are only three words in the English language that end with *ceed*: *exceed, proceed,* and *succeed*. There is only one word in the English language that ends with *sede*: *supersede*. Most other words that sound like *sede* or *ceed* end with *cede*. The following are examples:

- concede, recede, and precede

Words Ending in able or ible

For words ending in *able* or *ible*, there are no hard and fast rules. The following are examples:

- adjustable, unbeatable, collectable, deliverable, and likeable
- edible, compatible, feasible, sensible, and credible

There are more words ending in *able* than *ible*; this is useful to know if guessing is necessary.

Words Ending in ance or ence

The suffixes *ence, ency,* and *ent* are used in the following cases:

- the suffix is preceded by the letter *c* but sounds like *s* – *innocence*
- the suffix is preceded by the letter *g* but sounds like *j* – *intelligence, negligence*

The suffixes *ance, ancy,* and *ant* are used in the following cases:

- the suffix is preceded by the letter *c* but sounds like *k* – *significant, vacant*
- the suffix is preceded by the letter *g* with a hard sound – *elegant, extravagance*

If the suffix is preceded by other letters, there are no clear rules. For example: *finance, abundance,* and *assistance* use the letter *a,* while *decadence, competence,* and *excellence* use the letter *e.*

Words Ending in tion, sion, or cian

Words ending in *tion, sion,* or *cian* all sound like *shun* or *zhun*. There are no rules for which ending is used for words. The following are examples:

- action, agitation, caution, fiction, nation, and motion
- admission, expression, mansion, permission, and television
- electrician, magician, musician, optician, and physician (note that these words tend to describe occupations)

Words with the ai or ia Combination

When deciding if *ai* or *ia* is correct, the combination of *ai* usually sounds like one vowel sound, as in *Britain*, while the vowels in *ia* are pronounced separately, as in *guardian*. The following are examples:

- captain, certain, faint, hair, malaise, and praise (*ai* makes one sound)
- bacteria, beneficiary, diamond, humiliation, and nuptial (*ia* makes two sounds)

Rules for Plurals

Nouns Ending in ch, sh, s, x, or z

When a noun ends in the letters *ch, sh, s, x,* or *z*, an *es* instead of a singular *s* is added to the end of the word to make it plural. The following are examples:

- church becomes churches
- bush becomes bushes
- bass becomes basses
- mix becomes mixes
- buzz becomes buzzes

This is the rule with proper names as well; the Ross family would become the Rosses.

Nouns Ending in y or ay/ey/iy/oy/uy

If a noun ends with a **consonant and y**, the plural is formed by replacing the *y* with *ies*. For example, *fly* becomes *flies* and *puppy* becomes *puppies*. If a noun ends with a **vowel and *y***, the plural is formed by adding an *s*. For example, *alley* becomes *alleys* and *boy* becomes *boys*.

Nouns Ending in f or fe

Most nouns ending in *f* or *fe* are pluralized by replacing the *f* with *v* and adding *es*. The following are examples:

- knife becomes knives; self becomes selves; wolf becomes wolves.

An exception to this rule is the word *roof; roof* becomes *roofs*.

Nouns Ending in o

Most nouns ending with a **consonant and *o*** are pluralized by adding *es*. The following are examples:

- hero becomes heroes; tornado becomes tornadoes; potato becomes potatoes

Most nouns ending with a **vowel and *o*** are pluralized by adding *s*. The following are examples:

- portfolio becomes portfolios; radio becomes radios; cameo becomes cameos.

An exception to these rules is seen with musical terms ending in *o*. These words are pluralized by adding *s* even if they end in a consonant and *o*. The following are examples: *soprano* becomes *sopranos; banjo* becomes *banjos; piano* becomes *pianos.*

Letters, Numbers, and Symbols

Letters and numbers become plural by adding an apostrophe and *s*. The following are examples:

- The *L's* are the people whose names begin with the letter *L*.
- They broke the teams down into groups of *3's*.
- The sorority girls were all *KD's*.

Compound Nouns

A **compound noun** is a noun that is made up of two or more words; they can be written with hyphens. For example, *mother-in-law* or *court-martial* are compound nouns. To make them plural, an *s* or *es* is added to the noun portion of the word. The following are examples: *mother-in-law* becomes *mothers-in-law; court-martial* becomes *courts-martial.*

Exceptions

Some words do not fall into any specific category for making the singular form plural. They are **irregular**. Certain words become plural by changing the vowels within the word. The following are examples:

- woman becomes women; goose becomes geese; foot becomes feet

Some words change in unusual ways in the plural form. The following are examples:

- mouse becomes mice; ox becomes oxen; person becomes people

Some words are the same in both the singular and plural forms. The following are examples:

- *Salmon*, *deer*, and *moose* are the same whether singular or plural.

Commonly Misspelled Words

accidentally	accommodate	accompanied	accompany
achieved	acknowledgment	across	address
aggravate	aisle	ancient	anxiety
apparently	appearance	arctic	argument
arrangement	attendance	auxiliary	awkward
bachelor	barbarian	beggar	beneficiary
biscuit	brilliant	business	cafeteria
calendar	campaign	candidate	ceiling
cemetery	changeable	changing	characteristic
chauffeur	colonel	column	commit
committee	comparative	compel	competent
competition	conceive	congratulations	conqueror
conscious	coolly	correspondent	courtesy
curiosity	cylinder	deceive	deference

deferred	definite	describe	desirable
desperate	develop	diphtheria	disappear
disappoint	disastrous	discipline	discussion
disease	dissatisfied	dissipate	drudgery
ecstasy	efficient	eighth	eligible
embarrass	emphasize	especially	exaggerate
exceed	exhaust	exhilaration	existence
explanation	extraordinary	familiar	fascinate
February	fiery	finally	forehead
foreign	foreigner	foremost	forfeit
ghost	glamorous	government	grammar
grateful	grief	grievous	handkerchief
harass	height	hoping	hurriedly
hygiene	hypocrisy	imminent	incidentally
incredible	independent	indigestible	inevitable
innocence	intelligible	intentionally	intercede
interest	irresistible	judgment	legitimate
liable	library	likelihood	literature
maintenance	maneuver	manual	mathematics
mattress	miniature	mischievous	misspell
momentous	mortgage	neither	nickel
niece	ninety	noticeable	notoriety
obedience	obstacle	occasion	occurrence
omitted	operate	optimistic	organization
outrageous	pageant	pamphlet	parallel
parliament	permissible	perseverance	persuade
physically	physician	possess	possibly
practically	prairie	preceding	prejudice
prevalent	professor	pronunciation	pronouncement
propeller	protein	psychiatrist	psychology
quantity	questionnaire	rally	recede
receive	recognize	recommend	referral
referred	relieve	religious	resistance
restaurant	rhetoric	rhythm	ridiculous
sacrilegious	salary	scarcely	schedule
secretary	sentinel	separate	severely
sheriff	shriek	similar	soliloquy
sophomore	species	strenuous	studying
suffrage	supersede	suppress	surprise
symmetry	temperament	temperature	tendency
tournament	tragedy	transferred	truly
twelfth	tyranny	unanimous	unpleasant
usage	vacuum	valuable	vein
vengeance	vigilance	villain	Wednesday
weird	wholly		

Vocabulary

Your vocabulary is simply all the words you understand and use. Knowing the meanings of a large number of words, and how to use them, is important for success in a career as a peace officer. You'll be communicating both in speech and in writing with your fellow officers, your superiors, and the general public. Not being able to understand what someone else means would be a serious roadblock to successfully carrying out your duties, as would not being able to communicate precisely and efficiently.

Word Roots and Prefixes and Suffixes

Affixes

Affixes in the English language are morphemes that are added to words to create related but different words. Derivational affixes form new words based on and related to the original words. For example, the affix *-ness* added to the end of the adjective *happy* forms the noun *happiness.* Inflectional affixes form different grammatical versions of words. For example, the plural affix *-s* changes the singular noun *book* to the plural noun *books,* and the past tense affix *-ed* changes the present tense verb *look* to the past tense *looked.* Prefixes are affixes placed in front of words. For example, *heat* means to make hot; *preheat* means to heat in advance. Suffixes are affixes placed at the ends of words. The *happiness* example above contains the suffix *-ness.* Circumfixes add parts both before and after words, such as how *light* becomes *enlighten* with the prefix *en-* and the suffix *-en.* Interfixes create compound words via central affixes: *speed* and *meter* become *speedometer* via the interfix *-o-*.

Review Video: Affixes
Visit mometrix.com/academy and enter code: 782422

Word Roots, Prefixes, and Suffixes to Help Determine Meanings of Words

Many English words were formed from combining multiple sources. For example, the Latin *habēre* means "to have," and the prefixes *in-* and *im-* mean a lack or prevention of something, as in *insufficient* and *imperfect.* Latin combined *in-* with *habēre* to form *inhibēre,* whose past participle was *inhibitus.* This is the origin of the English word *inhibit,* meaning to prevent from having. Hence by knowing the meanings of both the prefix and the root, one can decipher the word meaning. In Greek, the root *enkephalo-* refers to the brain. Many medical terms are based on this root, such as encephalitis and hydrocephalus. Understanding the prefix and suffix meanings (*-itis* means inflammation; *hydro-* means water) allows a person to deduce that encephalitis refers to brain inflammation and hydrocephalus refers to water (or other fluid) in the brain.

Review Video: Root Words in English
Visit mometrix.com/academy and enter code: 896380

Review Video: Determining Word Meanings
Visit mometrix.com/academy and enter code: 894894

Prefixes

While knowing prefix meanings helps ESL and beginning readers learn new words, other readers take for granted the meanings of known words. However, prefix knowledge will also benefit them for determining meanings or definitions of unfamiliar words. For example, native English speakers and readers familiar with recipes know what *preheat* means. Knowing that *pre-* means in advance can also inform them that *presume* means to assume in advance, that *prejudice* means advance judgment, and that this understanding can be applied to many other words beginning with *pre-*.

Knowing that the prefix *dis-* indicates opposition informs the meanings of words like *disbar, disagree, disestablish,* and many more. Knowing *dys-* means bad, impaired, abnormal, or difficult informs *dyslogistic, dysfunctional, dysphagia,* and *dysplasia.*

SUFFIXES

In English, certain suffixes generally indicate both that a word is a noun, and that the noun represents a state of being or quality. For example, *-ness* is commonly used to change an adjective into its noun form, as with *happy* and *happiness, nice* and *niceness,* and so on. The suffix *–tion* is commonly used to transform a verb into its noun form, as with *converse* and *conversation or move* and *motion.* Thus, if readers are unfamiliar with the second form of a word, knowing the meaning of the transforming suffix can help them determine meaning.

PREFIXES FOR NUMBERS

Prefix	Definition	Examples
bi-	two	bisect, biennial
mono-	one, single	monogamy, monologue
poly-	many	polymorphous, polygamous
semi-	half, partly	semicircle, semicolon
uni-	one	uniform, unity

Prefixes for Time, Direction, and Space

Prefix	Definition	Examples
a-	in, on, of, up, to	abed, afoot
ab-	from, away, off	abdicate, abjure
ad-	to, toward	advance, adventure
ante-	before, previous	antecedent, antedate
anti-	against, opposing	antipathy, antidote
cata-	down, away, thoroughly	catastrophe, cataclysm
circum-	around	circumspect, circumference
com-	with, together, very	commotion, complicate
contra-	against, opposing	contradict, contravene
de-	from	depart
dia-	through, across, apart	diameter, diagnose
dis-	away, off, down, not	dissent, disappear
epi-	upon	epilogue
ex-	out	extract, excerpt
hypo-	under, beneath	hypodermic, hypothesis
inter-	among, between	intercede, interrupt
intra-	within	intramural, intrastate
ob-	against, opposing	objection
per-	through	perceive, permit
peri-	around	periscope, perimeter
post-	after, following	postpone, postscript
pre-	before, previous	prevent, preclude
pro-	forward, in place of	propel, pronoun
retro-	back, backward	retrospect, retrograde
sub-	under, beneath	subjugate, substitute
super-	above, extra	supersede, supernumerary
trans-	across, beyond, over	transact, transport
ultra-	beyond, excessively	ultramodern, ultrasonic

Negative Prefixes

Prefix	Definition	Examples
a-	without, lacking	atheist, agnostic
in-	not, opposing	incapable, ineligible
non-	not	nonentity, nonsense
un-	not, reverse of	unhappy, unlock

Extra Prefixes

Prefix	Definition	Examples
for-	away, off, from	forget, forswear
fore-	previous	foretell, forefathers
homo-	same, equal	homogenized, homonym
hyper-	excessive, over	hypercritical, hypertension
in-	in, into	intrude, invade
mal-	bad, poorly, not	malfunction, malpractice
mis-	bad, poorly, not	misspell, misfire
neo-	new	Neolithic, neoconservative
omni-	all, everywhere	omniscient, omnivore
ortho-	right, straight	orthogonal, orthodox
over-	above	overbearing, oversight
pan-	all, entire	panorama, pandemonium
para-	beside, beyond	parallel, paradox
re-	backward, again	revoke, recur
sym-	with, together	sympathy, symphony

Below is a list of common suffixes and their meanings:

Adjective Suffixes

Suffix	Definition	Examples
-able (-ible)	capable of being	toler*able*, ed*ible*
-esque	in the style of, like	picturesque, grotesque
-ful	filled with, marked by	thankful, zestful
-ific	make, cause	terrific, beatific
-ish	suggesting, like	churlish, childish
-less	lacking, without	hopeless, countless
-ous	marked by, given to	religious, riotous

Noun Suffixes

Suffix	Definition	Examples
-acy	state, condition	accuracy, privacy
-ance	act, condition, fact	acceptance, vigilance
-ard	one that does excessively	drunkard, sluggard
-ation	action, state, result	occupation, starvation
-dom	state, rank, condition	serfdom, wisdom
-er (-or)	office, action	teach*er*, elevat*or*, hon*or*
-ess	feminine	waitress, duchess
-hood	state, condition	manhood, statehood
-ion	action, result, state	union, fusion
-ism	act, manner, doctrine	barbarism, socialism
-ist	worker, follower	monopolist, socialist
-ity (-ty)	state, quality, condition	acid*ity*, civil*ity*, twen*ty*
-ment	result, action	Refreshment
-ness	quality, state	greatness, tallness
-ship	position	internship, statesmanship
-sion (-tion)	state, result	revi*sion*, expedi*tion*
-th	act, state, quality	warmth, width
-tude	quality, state, result	magnitude, fortitude

Verb Suffixes

Suffix	Definition	Examples
-ate	having, showing	separate, desolate
-en	cause to be, become	deepen, strengthen
-fy	make, cause to have	glorify, fortify
-ize	cause to be, treat with	sterilize, mechanize

Determining Word Meanings

Synonyms and Antonyms

When you understand how words relate to each other, you will discover more in a passage. This is explained by understanding **synonyms** (e.g., words that mean the same thing) and **antonyms** (e.g., words that mean the opposite of one another). As an example, *dry* and *arid* are synonyms, and *dry* and *wet* are antonyms.

There are many pairs of words in English that can be considered synonyms, despite having slightly different definitions. For instance, the words *friendly* and *collegial* can both be used to describe a warm interpersonal relationship, and one would be correct to call them synonyms. However, *collegial* (kin to *colleague*) is often used in reference to professional or academic relationships, and *friendly* has no such connotation.

If the difference between the two words is too great, then they should not be called synonyms. *Hot* and *warm* are not synonyms because their meanings are too distinct. A good way to determine whether two words are synonyms is to substitute one word for the other word and verify that the meaning of the sentence has not changed. Substituting *warm* for *hot* in a sentence would convey a different meaning. Although warm and hot may seem close in meaning, warm generally means that the temperature is moderate, and hot generally means that the temperature is excessively high.

Antonyms are words with opposite meanings. *Light* and *dark*, *up* and *down*, *right* and *left*, *good* and *bad*: these are all sets of antonyms. Be careful to distinguish between antonyms and pairs of words that are simply different. *Black* and *gray*, for instance, are not antonyms because gray is not the opposite of black. *Black* and *white*, on the other hand, are antonyms.

Not every word has an antonym. For instance, many nouns do not. What would be the antonym of *chair*? During your exam, the questions related to antonyms are more likely to concern adjectives. You will recall that adjectives are words that describe a noun. Some common adjectives include *purple*, *fast*, *skinny*, and *sweet*. From those four adjectives, *purple* is the item that lacks a group of obvious antonyms.

Review Video: Synonyms and Antonyms
Visit mometrix.com/academy and enter code: 105612

Context Clues

Readers of all levels will encounter words that they have either never seen or have encountered only on a limited basis. The best way to define a word in **context** is to look for nearby words that can assist in revealing the meaning of the word. For instance, unfamiliar nouns are often accompanied by examples that provide a definition. Consider the following sentence: *Dave arrived at the party in hilarious garb: a leopard-print shirt, buckskin trousers, and bright green sneakers.* If a reader was unfamiliar with the meaning of garb, he or she could read the examples (i.e., a leopard-print shirt, buckskin trousers, and bright green sneakers) and quickly determine that the word means *clothing*. Examples will not always be this obvious. Consider this sentence: *Parsley, lemon, and flowers were just a few of the items he used as garnishes.* Here, the word *garnishes* is exemplified by parsley, lemon, and flowers. Readers who have eaten in a variety of restaurants will probably be able to identify a garnish as something used to decorate a plate.

Review Video: Reading Comprehension: Using Context Clues
Visit mometrix.com/academy and enter code: 613660

Using Contrast in Context Clues

In addition to looking at the context of a passage, readers can use contrast to define an unfamiliar word in context. In many sentences, the author will not describe the unfamiliar word directly; instead, he or she will describe the opposite of the unfamiliar word. Thus, you are provided with some information that will bring you closer to defining the word. Consider the following example: *Despite his intelligence, Hector's low brow and bad posture made him look obtuse.* The author writes that Hector's appearance does not convey intelligence. Therefore, *obtuse* must mean unintelligent. Here is another example: *Despite the horrible weather, we were beatific about our trip to Alaska.* The word *despite* indicates that the speaker's feelings were at odds with the weather. Since the weather is described as *horrible*, then *beatific* must mean something positive.

Substitution to Find Meaning

In some cases, there will be very few contextual clues to help a reader define the meaning of an unfamiliar word. When this happens, one strategy that readers may employ is **substitution**. A good reader will brainstorm some possible synonyms for the given word, and he or she will substitute these words into the sentence. If the sentence and the surrounding passage continue to make sense, then the substitution has revealed at least some information about the unfamiliar word. Consider the sentence: *Frank's admonition rang in her ears as she climbed the mountain.* A reader unfamiliar with *admonition* might come up with some substitutions like *vow*, *promise*, *advice*, *complaint*, or *compliment*. All of these words make general sense of the sentence, though their meanings are diverse. However, this process has suggested that an admonition is some sort of message. The substitution strategy is rarely able to pinpoint a precise definition, but this process can be effective as a last resort.

Occasionally, you will be able to define an unfamiliar word by looking at the descriptive words in the context. Consider the following sentence: *Fred dragged the recalcitrant boy kicking and screaming up the stairs.* The words *dragged*, *kicking*, and *screaming* all suggest that the boy does not want to go up the stairs. The reader may assume that *recalcitrant* means something like unwilling or protesting. In this example, an unfamiliar adjective was identified.

Additionally, using description to define an unfamiliar noun is a common practice compared to unfamiliar adjectives, as in this sentence: *Don's wrinkled frown and constantly shaking fist identified him as a curmudgeon of the first order.* Don is described as having a *wrinkled frown and constantly shaking fist*, suggesting that a *curmudgeon* must be a grumpy person. Contrasts do not always provide detailed information about the unfamiliar word, but they at least give the reader some clues.

Words with Multiple Meanings

When a word has more than one meaning, readers can have difficulty determining how the word is being used in a given sentence. For instance, the verb *cleave*, can mean either *join* or *separate*. When readers come upon this word, they will have to select the definition that makes the most sense. Consider the following sentence: *Hermione's knife cleaved the bread cleanly.* Since a knife cannot join bread together, the word must indicate separation. A slightly more difficult example would be the sentence: *The birds cleaved to one another as they flew from the oak tree.* Immediately, the presence of the words *to one another* should suggest that in this sentence *cleave* is being used to mean *join*. Discovering the intent of a word with multiple meanings requires the same tricks as defining an unknown word: look for contextual clues and evaluate the substituted words.

Syntax to Determine Part of Speech and Meanings of Words

Syntax refers to sentence structure and word order. Suppose that a reader encounters an unfamiliar word when reading a text. To illustrate, consider an invented word like "splunch." If this word is used in a sentence like "Please splunch that ball to me," the reader can assume from syntactic context that "splunch" is a verb. We would not use a noun, adjective, adverb, or preposition with the object "that ball," and the prepositional phrase "to me" further indicates "splunch" represents an action. However, in the sentence, "Please hand that splunch to me," the reader can assume that "splunch" is a noun. Demonstrative adjectives like "that" modify nouns. Also, we hand someone some*thing*—a thing being a noun; we do not hand someone a verb, adjective, or adverb. Some sentences contain further clues. For example, from the sentence, "The princess wore the glittering splunch on her head," the reader can deduce that it is a crown, tiara, or something similar from the syntactic context, without knowing the word.

Reading Ability

Reading Comprehension

For all peace officers, reading is an important part of the job and reading comprehension skills are critical to your success in this occupation. Whether you're reading memos, reports, rules and regulations, or any of the many other kinds of reading material you'll encounter on your job, it's imperative that you have the ability to understand and process the material. While these abilities are necessary for everyone working in law enforcement, anyone who wants to be promoted to higher positions in this field must have extremely strong reading comprehension skills.

Identifying Topics and Main Ideas

One of the most important skills in reading comprehension is the identification of **topics** and **main ideas**. There is a subtle difference between these two features. The topic is the subject of a text (i.e., what the text is all about). The main idea, on the other hand, is the most important point being made by the author. The topic is usually expressed in a few words at the most while the main idea often needs a full sentence to be completely defined. As an example, a short passage might be written on the topic of penguins, and the main idea could be written as *Penguins are different from other birds in many ways*. In most nonfiction writing, the topic and the main idea will be **stated directly** and often appear in a sentence at the very beginning or end of the text. When being tested on an understanding of the author's topic, you may be able to skim the passage for the general idea by reading only the first sentence of each paragraph. A body paragraph's first sentence is often—but not always—the main **topic sentence** which gives you a summary of the content in the paragraph.

However, there are cases in which the reader must figure out an **unstated** topic or main idea. In these instances, you must read every sentence of the text and try to come up with an overarching idea that is supported by each of those sentences.

Note: The main idea should not be confused with the thesis statement. While the main idea gives a brief, general summary of a text, the thesis statement provides a **specific perspective** on an issue that the author supports with evidence.

Review Video: Topics and Main Ideas
Visit mometrix.com/academy and enter code: 407801

Supporting Details

Supporting details are smaller pieces of evidence that provide backing for the main point. In order to show that a main idea is correct or valid, an author must add details that prove their point. All texts contain details, but they are only classified as supporting details when they serve to reinforce some larger point. Supporting details are most commonly found in informative and persuasive texts. In some cases, they will be clearly indicated with terms like *for example* or *for instance*, or they will be enumerated with terms like *first, second*, and *last*. However, you need to be prepared for texts that do not contain those indicators. As a reader, you should consider whether the author's supporting details really back up his or her main point. Details can be factual and correct, yet they may not be **relevant** to the author's point. Conversely, details can be relevant, but be ineffective because they are based on opinion or assertions that cannot be proven.

Review Video: Supporting Details
Visit mometrix.com/academy and enter code: 396297

An example of a main idea is: *Giraffes live in the Serengeti of Africa*. A supporting detail about giraffes could be: *A giraffe in this region benefits from a long neck by reaching twigs and leaves on tall trees.* The main idea gives the general idea that the text is about giraffes. The supporting detail gives a specific fact about how the giraffes eat.

Making Predictions

A **prediction** is a guess about what will happen next. Readers constantly make predictions based on what they have read and what they already know. We can make predictions before we begin reading and during our reading. Consider the following sentence: *Staring at the computer screen in shock, Kim blindly reached over for the brimming glass of water on the shelf to her side.* The sentence suggests that Kim is distracted, and that she is not looking at the glass that she is going to pick up. So, a reader might predict that Kim is going to knock over the glass. Of course, not every prediction will be accurate: perhaps Kim will pick the glass up cleanly. Nevertheless, the author has certainly created the expectation that the water might be spilled.

As we read on, we can test the accuracy of our predictions, revise them in light of additional reading, and confirm or refute our predictions. Predictions are always subject to revision as the reader acquires more information. A reader can make predictions by observing the title and illustrations; noting the structure, characters, and subject; drawing on existing knowledge relative to the subject; and asking "why" and "who" questions. Connecting reading to what we already know enables us to learn new information and construct meaning. Activating existing background knowledge and thinking about the text before reading improves comprehension.

Review Video: Predictive Reading
Visit mometrix.com/academy and enter code: 437248

Test-taking tip: To respond to questions requiring future predictions, your answers should be based on evidence of past or present behavior and events.

Inferences

Inferences are logical conclusions that readers make based on their observations and previous knowledge. An inference is based on both what is found in a passage or a story and what is known from personal experience. For instance, a story may say that a character is frightened and can hear howling in the distance. Based on both what is in the text and personal knowledge, it is a logical conclusion that the character is frightened because he hears the sound of wolves. A good inference is supported by the information in a passage.

Implicit and Explicit Information

By inferring, readers construct meanings from text that are personally relevant. By combining their own schemas or concepts and their background information pertinent to the text with what they read, readers interpret it according to both what the author has conveyed and their own unique perspectives. Inferences are different from **explicit information**, which is clearly stated in a passage. Authors do not always explicitly spell out every meaning in what they write; many meanings are implicit. Through inference, readers can comprehend implied meanings in the text, and also derive personal significance from it, making the text meaningful and memorable to them. Inference is a natural process in everyday life. When readers infer, they can draw conclusions about what the author is saying, predict what may reasonably follow, amend these predictions as they continue to read, interpret the import of themes, and analyze the characters' feelings and motivations through their actions.

Example of Drawing Conclusions from Inferences

Read the excerpt and decide why Jana finally relaxed.

> Jana loved her job, but the work was very demanding. She had trouble relaxing. She called a friend, but she still thought about work. She ordered a pizza, but eating it did not help. Then, her kitten jumped on her lap and began to purr. Jana leaned back and began to hum a little tune. She felt better.

You can draw the conclusion that Jana relaxed because her kitten jumped on her lap. The kitten purred, and Jana leaned back and hummed a tune. Then she felt better. The excerpt does not explicitly say that this is the reason why she was able to relax. The text leaves the matter unclear, but the reader can infer or make a "best guess" that this is the reason she is relaxing. This is a logical conclusion based on the information in the passage. It is the best conclusion a reader can make based on the information he or she has read. Inferences are based on the information in a passage, but they are not directly stated in the passage.

Test-taking tip: While being tested on your ability to make correct inferences, you must look for **contextual clues**. An answer can be true, but not the best or most correct answer. The contextual clues will help you find the answer that is the **best answer** out of the given choices. Be careful in your reading to understand the context in which a phrase is stated. When asked for the implied meaning of a statement made in the passage, you should immediately locate the statement and read the **context** in which the statement was made. Also, look for an answer choice that has a similar phrase to the statement in question.

Review Video: Inference
Visit mometrix.com/academy and enter code: 379203

Organization of the Text

The way a text is organized can help readers understand the author's intent and his or her conclusions. There are various ways to organize a text, and each one has a purpose and use. Usually, authors will organize information logically in a passage so the reader can follow and locate the information within the text. However, since not all passages are written with the same logical structure, you need to be familiar with several different types of passage structure.

Chronological

When using **chronological** order, the author presents information in the order that it happened. For example, biographies are typically written in chronological order. The subject's birth and childhood are presented first, followed by their adult life, and lastly the events leading up to the person's death.

Cause and Effect

One of the most common text structures is **cause and effect**. A **cause** is an act or event that makes something happen, and an **effect** is the thing that happens as a result of the cause. A cause-and-effect relationship is not always explicit, but there are some terms in English that signal causes, such as *since*, *because*, and *due to*. Furthermore, terms that signal effects include *consequently, therefore, this leads to*. As an example, consider the sentence *Because the sky was clear, Ron did not bring an umbrella*. The cause is the clear sky, and the effect is that Ron did not bring an umbrella. However, readers may find that sometimes the cause-and-effect relationship will not be clearly noted. For instance, the sentence *He was late and missed the meeting* does not contain any signaling words, but the sentence still contains a cause (he was late) and an effect (he missed the meeting).

Review Video: Cause and Effect
Visit mometrix.com/academy and enter code: 868099

Multiple Effects

Be aware of the possibility for a single cause to have **multiple effects.** (e.g., *Single cause*: Because you left your homework on the table, your dog engulfed the assignment. *Multiple effects*: As a result, you receive a failing grade, your parents do not allow you to go out with your friends, you miss out on the new movie, and one of your classmates spoils it for you before you have another chance to watch it).

Multiple Causes

Also, there is the possibility for a single effect to have **multiple causes.** (e.g., *Single effect*: Alan has a fever. *Multiple causes*: An unexpected cold front came through the area, and Alan forgot to take his multi-vitamin to avoid getting sick.) Additionally, an effect can in turn be the cause of another effect, in what is known as a cause-and-effect chain. (e.g., As a result of her disdain for procrastination, Lynn prepared for her exam. This led to her passing her test with high marks. Hence, her resume was accepted and her application was approved.)

Cause and Effect in Persuasive Essays

Persuasive essays, in which an author tries to make a convincing argument and change the minds of readers, usually include cause-and-effect relationships. However, these relationships should not always be taken at face value. Frequently, an author will assume a cause or take an effect for granted. To read a persuasive essay effectively, readers need to judge the cause-and-effect relationships that the author is presenting. For instance, imagine an author wrote the following: *The parking deck has been unprofitable because people would prefer to ride their bikes.* The relationship is clear: the cause is that people prefer to ride their bikes, and the effect is that the parking deck has been unprofitable. However, readers should consider whether this argument is conclusive. Perhaps there are other reasons for the failure of the parking deck: a down economy, excessive fees, etc. Too often, authors present causal relationships as if they are fact rather than opinion. Readers should be on the alert for these dubious claims.

Problem-Solution

Some nonfiction texts are organized to **present a problem** followed by a solution. For this type of text, the problem is often explained before the solution is offered. In some cases, as when the problem is well known, the solution may be introduced briefly at the beginning. Other passages may focus on the solution, and the problem will be referenced only occasionally. Some texts will outline multiple solutions to a problem, leaving readers to choose among them. If the author has an interest or an allegiance to one solution, he or she may fail to mention or describe accurately some of the other solutions. Readers should be careful of the author's agenda when reading a problem-solution text. Only by understanding the author's perspective and interests can one develop a proper judgment of the proposed solution.

Compare and Contrast

Many texts follow the **compare-and-contrast** model in which the similarities and differences between two ideas or things are explored. Analysis of the similarities between ideas is called **comparison**. In an ideal comparison, the author places ideas or things in an equivalent structure, i.e., the author presents the ideas in the same way. If an author wants to show the similarities between cricket and baseball, then he or she may do so by summarizing the equipment and rules for each game. Be mindful of the similarities as they appear in the passage and take note of any differences that are mentioned. Often, these small differences will only reinforce the more general similarity.

Review Video: Compare and Contrast
Visit mometrix.com/academy and enter code: 798319

Thinking critically about ideas and conclusions can seem like a daunting task. One way to ease this task is to understand the basic elements of ideas and writing techniques. Looking at the ways different ideas relate to each other can be a good way for readers to begin their analysis. For instance, sometimes authors will write about two ideas that are in opposition to each other. Or, one author will provide his or her ideas on a topic, and another author may respond in opposition. The analysis of these opposing ideas is known as **contrast**. Contrast is often marred by the author's obvious partiality to one of the ideas. A discerning reader will be put off by an author who does not engage in a fair fight. In an analysis of opposing ideas, both ideas should be presented in clear and reasonable terms. If the author does prefer a side, you need to read carefully to determine the areas where the author shows or avoids this preference. In an analysis of opposing ideas, you should proceed through the passage by marking the major differences point by point with an eye that is looking for an explanation of each side's view. For instance, in an analysis of capitalism and communism, there is an importance in outlining each side's view on labor, markets, prices, personal responsibility, etc. Additionally, as you read through the passages, you should note whether the opposing views present each side in a similar manner.

Sequence

Readers must be able to identify a text's **sequence**, or the order in which things happen. Often, when the sequence is very important to the author, the text is indicated with signal words like *first, then, next,* and *last.* However, a sequence can be merely implied and must be noted by the reader. Consider the sentence *He walked through the garden and gave water and fertilizer to the plants.* Clearly, the man did not walk through the garden before he collected water and fertilizer for the plants. So, the implied sequence is that he first collected water, then he collected fertilizer, next he walked through the garden, and last he gave water or fertilizer as necessary to the plants. Texts do not always proceed in an orderly sequence from first to last. Sometimes they begin at the end and start over at the beginning. As a reader, you can enhance your understanding of the passage by taking brief notes to clarify the sequence.

Review Video: Sequence
Visit mometrix.com/academy and enter code: 489027

TRANSITIONS

Transitions between sentences and paragraphs guide readers from idea to idea and indicate relationships between sentences and paragraphs. Writers should be judicious in their use of transitions, inserting them sparingly. They should also be selected to fit the author's purpose—transitions can indicate time, comparison, and conclusion, among other purposes. Tone is also important to consider when using transitional phrases, varying the tone for different audiences. For example, in a scholarly essay, *in summary* would be preferable to the more informal *in short*.

When working with transitional words and phrases, writers usually find a natural flow that indicates when a transition is needed. In reading a draft of the text, it should become apparent where the flow is disrupted. At this point, the writer can add transitional elements during the revision process. Revising can also afford an opportunity to delete transitional devices that seem heavy handed or unnecessary.

Review Video: Transitions in Writing
Visit mometrix.com/academy and enter code: 233246

TYPES OF TRANSITIONAL WORDS

Time	Afterward, immediately, earlier, meanwhile, recently, lately, now, since, soon, when, then, until, before, etc.
Sequence	too, first, second, further, moreover, also, again, and, next, still, besides, finally
Comparison	similarly, in the same way, likewise, also, again, once more
Contrasting	but, although, despite, however, instead, nevertheless, on the one hand... on the other hand, regardless, yet, in contrast
Cause and Effect	because, consequently, thus, therefore, then, to this end, since, so, as a result, if... then, accordingly
Examples	for example, for instance, such as, to illustrate, indeed, in fact, specifically
Place	near, far, here, there, to the left/right, next to, above, below, beyond, opposite, beside
Concession	granted that, naturally, of course, it may appear, although it is true that
Repetition, Summary, or Conclusion	as mentioned earlier, as noted, in other words, in short, on the whole, to summarize, therefore, as a result, to conclude, in conclusion
Addition	and, also, furthermore, moreover
Generalization	in broad terms, broadly speaking, in general

Cloze Test

A cloze test is a kind of reading test that measures how well you comprehend what you're reading, and also your ability to understand the context of what you're reading. It consists of a reading passage in which several words have been removed. In place of each removed word, there are a series of blank spaces indicating how many letters the removed word had. You must determine what word belongs in each set of blank spaces.

Review the following parts of speech to prepare for this sub-test of Reading Ability.

Parts of Speech

Nouns

A noun is a person, place, thing, or idea. The two main types of nouns are **common** and **proper** nouns. Nouns can also be categorized as abstract (i.e., general) or concrete (i.e., specific).

Common Nouns

Common nouns are generic names for people, places, and things. Common nouns are not usually capitalized.

Examples of common nouns:

People: boy, girl, worker, manager

Places: school, bank, library, home

Things: dog, cat, truck, car

Review Video: Nouns
Visit mometrix.com/academy and enter code: 344028

Proper Nouns

Proper nouns name specific people, places, or things. All proper nouns are capitalized.

Examples of proper nouns:

People: Abraham Lincoln, George Washington, Martin Luther King, Jr.

Places: Los Angeles, California; New York; Asia

Things: Statue of Liberty, Earth, Lincoln Memorial

Note: Some nouns can be either common or proper depending on their use. For example, when referring to the planet that we live on, *Earth* is a proper noun and is capitalized. When referring to the dirt, rocks, or land on our planet, *earth* is a common noun and is not capitalized.

General and Specific Nouns

General nouns are the names of conditions or ideas. **Specific nouns** name people, places, and things that are understood by using your senses.

General nouns:

Condition: beauty, strength

Idea: truth, peace

Specific nouns:

People: baby, friend, father

Places: town, park, city hall

Things: rainbow, cough, apple, silk, gasoline

COLLECTIVE NOUNS

Collective nouns are the names for a group of people, places, or things that may act as a whole. The following are examples of collective nouns: *class, company, dozen, group, herd, team,* and *public*. Collective nouns usually require an article, which denotes the noun as being a single unit. For instance, a choir is a group of singers. Even though there are many singers in a choir, the word choir is grammatically treated as a single unit. If we refer to the members of the group, and not the group itself, it is no longer a collective noun.

Incorrect: The *choir are* going to compete nationally this year.

Correct: The *choir is* going to compete nationally this year.

Incorrect: The *members* of the choir *is* competing nationally this year.

Correct: The *members* of the choir *are* competing nationally this year.

PRONOUNS

Pronouns are words that are used to stand in for nouns. A pronoun may be classified as personal, intensive, relative, interrogative, demonstrative, indefinite, and reciprocal.

Personal: *Nominative* is the case for nouns and pronouns that are the subject of a sentence. *Objective* is the case for nouns and pronouns that are an object in a sentence. *Possessive* is the case for nouns and pronouns that show possession or ownership.

Singular

	Nominative	Objective	Possessive
First Person	I	me	my, mine
Second Person	you	you	your, yours
Third Person	he, she, it	him, her, it	his, her, hers, its

Plural

	Nominative	Objective	Possessive
First Person	we	us	our, ours
Second Person	you	you	your, yours
Third Person	they	them	their, theirs

Intensive: I myself, you yourself, he himself, she herself, the (thing) itself, we ourselves, you yourselves, they themselves

Relative: which, who, whom, whose

Interrogative: what, which, who, whom, whose

Demonstrative: this, that, these, those

Indefinite: all, any, each, everyone, either/neither, one, some, several

Reciprocal: each other, one another

Review Video: Nouns and Pronouns
Visit mometrix.com/academy and enter code: 312073

Verbs

A verb is a word or group of words that indicates action or being. In other words, the verb shows something's action or state of being or the action that has been done to something. If you want to write a sentence, then you need a verb. Without a verb, you have no sentence.

Transitive and Intransitive Verbs

A **transitive verb** is a verb whose action indicates a receiver. **Intransitive verbs** do not indicate a receiver of an action. In other words, the action of the verb does not point to an object.

Transitive: He drives a car. | She feeds the dog.

Intransitive: He runs every day. | She voted in the last election.

A dictionary will tell you whether a verb is transitive or intransitive. Some verbs can be transitive or intransitive.

Action Verbs and Linking Verbs

Action verbs show what the subject is doing. In other words, an action verb shows action. Unlike most types of words, a single action verb, in the right context, can be an entire sentence. **Linking verbs** link the subject of a sentence to a noun or pronoun, or they link a subject with an adjective. You always need a verb if you want a complete sentence. However, linking verbs on their own cannot be a complete sentence.

Common linking verbs include *appear, be, become, feel, grow, look, seem, smell, sound,* and *taste.* However, any verb that shows a condition and connects to a noun, pronoun, or adjective that describes the subject of a sentence is a linking verb.

Action: He sings. | Run! | Go! | I talk with him every day. | She reads.

Linking:

Incorrect: I am.

Correct: I am John. | The roses smell lovely. | I feel tired.

Note: Some verbs are followed by words that look like prepositions, but they are a part of the verb and a part of the verb's meaning. These are known as phrasal verbs, and examples include *call off*, *look up*, and *drop off*.

Review Video: Action Verbs and Linking Verbs
Visit mometrix.com/academy and enter code: 743142

VOICE

Transitive verbs may be in active voice or passive voice. The difference between active voice and passive voice is whether the subject is acting or being acted upon. When the subject of the sentence is doing the action, the verb is in **active voice**. When the subject is being acted upon, the verb is in **passive voice**.

Active: Jon drew the picture. (The subject *Jon* is doing the action of *drawing a picture.*)

Passive: The picture is drawn by Jon. (The subject *picture* is receiving the action from Jon.)

VERB TENSES

Verb **tense** is a property of a verb that indicates when the action being described takes place (past, present, or future) and whether or not the action is completed (simple or perfect). Describing an action taking place in the present (*I talk*) requires a different verb tense than describing an action that took place in the past (*I talked*). Some verb tenses require an auxiliary (helping) verb. These helping verbs include *am, are, is* | *have, has, had* | *was, were, will* (or *shall*).

Present: I talk	Present perfect: I have talked
Past: I talked	Past perfect: I had talked
Future: I will talk	Future perfect: I will have talked

Present: The action is happening at the current time.

Example: He *walks* to the store every morning.

To show that something is happening right now, use the progressive present tense: I *am walking*.

Past: The action happened in the past.

Example: She *walked* to the store an hour ago.

Future: The action will happen later.

Example: I *will walk* to the store tomorrow.

Present perfect: The action started in the past and continues into the present or took place previously at an unspecified time.

Example: I *have walked* to the store three times today.

Past perfect: The action was completed at some point in the past. This tense is usually used to describe an action that was completed before some other reference time or event.

Example: I *had eaten* already before they arrived.

Future perfect: The action will be completed before some point in the future. This tense may be used to describe an action that has already begun or has yet to begin.

Example: The project *will have been completed* by the deadline.

Review Video: Present Perfect, Past Perfect, and Future Perfect Verb Tenses
Visit mometrix.com/academy and enter code: 269472

Conjugating Verbs

When you need to change the form of a verb, you are **conjugating** a verb. The key forms of a verb are present tense (sing/sings), past tense (sang), present participle (singing), and past participle (sung). By combining these forms with helping verbs, you can make almost any verb tense. The following table demonstrate some of the different ways to conjugate a verb:

Tense	First Person	Second Person	Third Person Singular	Third Person Plural
Simple Present	I sing	You sing	He, she, it sings	They sing
Simple Past	I sang	You sang	He, she, it sang	They sang
Simple Future	I will sing	You will sing	He, she, it will sing	They will sing
Present Progressive	I am singing	You are singing	He, she, it is singing	They are singing
Past Progressive	I was singing	You were singing	He, she, it was singing	They were singing
Present Perfect	I have sung	You have sung	He, she, it has sung	They have sung
Past Perfect	I had sung	You had sung	He, she, it had sung	They had sung

Mood

There are three **moods** in English: the indicative, the imperative, and the subjunctive.

The **indicative mood** is used for facts, opinions, and questions.

Fact: You can do this.

Opinion: I think that you can do this.

Question: Do you know that you can do this?

The **imperative** is used for orders or requests.

Order: You are going to do this!

Request: Will you do this for me?

The **subjunctive mood** is for wishes and statements that go against fact.

Wish: I wish that I were famous.

Statement against fact: If I were you, I would do this. (This goes against fact because I am not you. You have the chance to do this, and I do not have the chance.)

ADJECTIVES

An **adjective** is a word that is used to modify a noun or pronoun. An adjective answers a question: *Which one? What kind?* or *How many?* Usually, adjectives come before the words that they modify, but they may also come after a linking verb.

Which one? The *third* suit is my favorite.

What kind? This suit is *navy blue.*

How many? I am going to buy *four* pairs of socks to match the suit.

> **Review Video: Descriptive Text**
> Visit mometrix.com/academy and enter code: 174903

ARTICLES

Articles are adjectives that are used to distinguish nouns as definite or indefinite. *A*, *an*, and *the* are the only articles. **Definite** nouns are preceded by *the* and indicate a specific person, place, thing, or idea. **Indefinite** nouns are preceded by *a* or *an* and do not indicate a specific person, place, thing, or idea.

Note: *An* comes before words that start with a vowel sound. For example, "Are you going to get an **u**mbrella?"

Definite: I lost *the* bottle that belongs to me.

Indefinite: Does anyone have *a* bottle to share?

> **Review Video: Function of Articles in a Sentence**
> Visit mometrix.com/academy and enter code: 449383

COMPARISON WITH ADJECTIVES

Some adjectives are relative and other adjectives are absolute. Adjectives that are **relative** can show the comparison between things. **Absolute** adjectives can also show comparison, but they do so in a different way. Let's say that you are reading two books. You think that one book is perfect, and the other book is not exactly perfect. It is not possible for one book to be more perfect than the other. Either you think that the book is perfect, or you think that the book is imperfect. In this case, perfect and imperfect are absolute adjectives.

Relative adjectives will show the different **degrees** of something or someone to something else or someone else. The three degrees of adjectives include positive, comparative, and superlative.

The **positive** degree is the normal form of an adjective.

Example: This work is *difficult.* | She is *smart.*

The **comparative** degree compares one person or thing to another person or thing.

Example: This work is *more difficult* than your work. | She is *smarter* than me.

The **superlative** degree compares more than two people or things.

Example: This is the *most difficult* work of my life. | She is the *smartest* lady in school.

Review Video: Adjectives
Visit mometrix.com/academy and enter code: 470154

Adverbs

An **adverb** is a word that is used to **modify** a verb, an adjective, or another adverb. Usually, adverbs answer one of these questions: *When? Where? How?* and *Why?* The negatives *not* and *never* are considered adverbs. Adverbs that modify adjectives or other adverbs **strengthen** or **weaken** the words that they modify.

Examples:

He walks *quickly* through the crowd.

The water flows *smoothly* on the rocks.

Note: Adverbs are usually indicated by the morpheme *-ly*, which has been added to the root word. For instance, *quick* can be made into an adverb by adding *-ly* to construct *quickly*. Some words that end in *-ly* do not follow this rule and can behave as other parts of speech. Examples of adjectives ending in *-ly* include: *early, friendly, holy, lonely, silly*, and *ugly*. To know if a word that ends in *-ly* is an adjective or adverb, check your dictionary. Also, while many adverbs end in *-ly*, you need to remember that not all adverbs end in *-ly*.

Examples:

He is *never* angry.

You are *too* irresponsible to travel alone.

Review Video: Adverbs
Visit mometrix.com/academy and enter code: 713951

Review Video: Adverbs that Modify Adjectives
Visit mometrix.com/academy and enter code: 122570

Comparison with Adverbs

The rules for comparing adverbs are the same as the rules for adjectives.

The **positive** degree is the standard form of an adverb.

Example: He arrives *soon*. | She speaks *softly* to her friends.

The **comparative** degree compares one person or thing to another person or thing.

Example: He arrives *sooner* than Sarah. | She speaks *more softly* than him.

The **superlative** degree compares more than two people or things.

Example: He arrives *soonest* of the group. | She speaks the *most softly* of any of her friends.

PREPOSITIONS

A **preposition** is a word placed before a noun or pronoun that shows the relationship between that noun or pronoun and another word in the sentence.

Common prepositions:

about	before	during	on	under
after	beneath	for	over	until
against	between	from	past	up
among	beyond	in	through	with
around	by	of	to	within
at	down	off	toward	without

Examples:

The napkin is *in* the drawer.

The Earth rotates *around* the Sun.

The needle is *beneath* the haystack.

Can you find "me" *among* the words?

Review Video: Prepositions
Visit mometrix.com/academy and enter code: 946763

CONJUNCTIONS

Conjunctions join words, phrases, or clauses and they show the connection between the joined pieces. **Coordinating conjunctions** connect equal parts of sentences. **Correlative conjunctions** show the connection between pairs. **Subordinating conjunctions** join subordinate (i.e., dependent) clauses with independent clauses.

COORDINATING CONJUNCTIONS

The **coordinating conjunctions** include: *and, but, yet, or, nor, for,* and *so*

Examples:

The rock was small, *but* it was heavy.

She drove in the night, *and* he drove in the day.

Correlative Conjunctions

The **correlative conjunctions** are: *either...or* | *neither...nor* | *not only...but also*

Examples:

Either you are coming *or* you are staying.

He *not only* ran three miles *but also* swam 200 yards.

Review Video: Coordinating and Correlative Conjunctions
Visit mometrix.com/academy and enter code: 390329

Review Video: Adverb Equal Comparisons
Visit mometrix.com/academy and enter code: 231291

Subordinating Conjunctions

Common **subordinating conjunctions** include:

after	since	whenever
although	so that	where
because	unless	wherever
before	until	whether
in order that	when	while

Examples:

I am hungry *because* I did not eat breakfast.

He went home *when* everyone left.

Review Video: Subordinating Conjunctions
Visit mometrix.com/academy and enter code: 958913

Interjections

Interjections are words of exclamation (i.e., audible expression of great feeling) that are used alone or as a part of a sentence. Often, they are used at the beginning of a sentence for an introduction. Sometimes, they can be used in the middle of a sentence to show a change in thought or attitude.

Common Interjections: Hey! | Oh, | Ouch! | Please! | Wow!

EXAMPLES

You will need to use contextual clues to complete the sentences with the missing words. One strategy you may use is substitution. A good reader will brainstorm some possible words for the blank space, and he or she will substitute these words into the sentence. If the sentence and the surrounding passage continue to make sense, then the substitution has revealed the missing word. Be sure that the word you use occupies every provided space for a letter. If there are six blank spaces for the missing word, then you need a word with six letters.

EXAMPLE 1

The father ran to help the _ _ _ _ _ on the bike.

In this example, we see the connection between a father and someone riding a bike. You can tell from this example that the missing word is a noun that has five letters. To select a word for the blank, you need to think about the context of the sentence. A father is running to take care of someone on the bike. So, one possible choice is child. A father is teaching his child to ride a bike, and the child needs assistance. Another possible choice is woman. There are five letters in the word, and it makes sense at least in this sentence. To know which word to choose, you would need to focus on the whole paragraph that will be provided to you. Be sure that you don't focus only on the blank spaces to fill in with the correct number of letters. Take time to read the whole paragraph and think about the context.

EXAMPLE 2

The soldiers saluted their commander as _ _ _ entered the room.

In this example, we see the connection between soldiers and their commanding officer. You can tell from this example that the missing word is a pronoun that refers to either the soldiers or the commander. The only pronoun that would make sense in that position for the soldiers is *they*, but there are only three letters in the missing word, so it must be referring to the commander. We know that there is only one commander, so we are looking for a singular, third-person, personal pronoun: *he* or *she*. Since the missing word has three letters, the answer must be *she*.

Alternatively, if the passage had already given the name of the commander and it was three letters long (Ann, Bob, Kat, Ted, etc.), that would also be an acceptable response.

Reasoning Ability

*Please note that depending on which agency you apply for, this section may be excluded from the exam. The Writing Ability, Reading Ability, and CLOZE sections are guaranteed to appear, but the Reasoning Ability may or may not be on your version of the test. *

Reasoning

The reasoning sub-test uses the format of multiple-choice questions to determine if you will be able to understand a logical sequence of ideas. Most questions fall into a few categories. However, each question will present you with a set of information, expect you to determine patterns, and ask for information based on those patterns.

Comparative Values

In this type of problem, you will be given a few comparisons between people or objects. The question will ask you to order the people or objects from least to greatest or find the value of a specific person or object. The key to these problems is to create a hierarchy based on the provided relationships.

Example:

Oak, Pecan, Evergreen, and Maple trees are rated by popularity in neighborhoods. Oak ranks in between Maple and Pecan. Maple ranks higher than Pecan. Evergreen is rated lowest. Which tree is rated highest?

a. Pecan
b. Oak
c. Evergreen
d. Maple

The answer is D. Maple. Starting with the lowest of Evergreen, the next highly rated tree will be Pecan because Oak separates the other two, of which pecan is lower. Oak is lower than Maple. Maple is the highest rated tree.

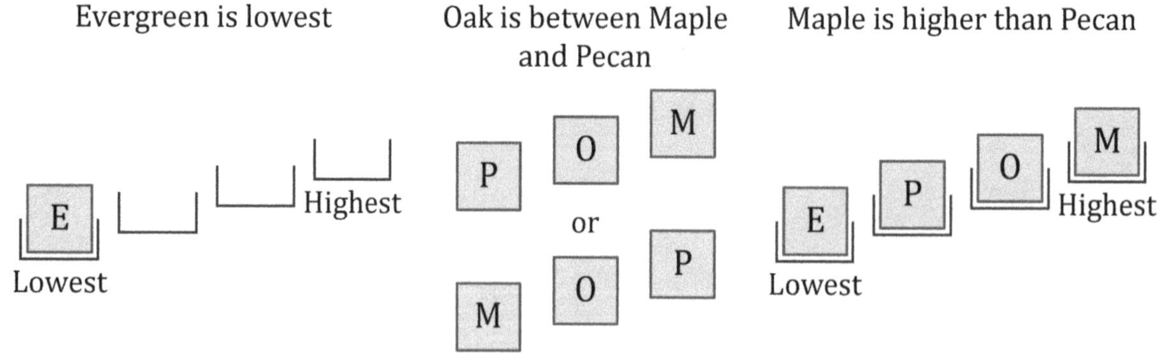

Numerical Series

In this type of problem, you will be given a set of numbers in a specific order. The question will ask you to find the value of the next number. The key to these problems is to check for constant increase/decrease, which could indicate adding or multiplying each number by another number, or check for repetition.

Example:

Identify the next number in the series: 5, 4, 3, 5, 4...

a. 2
b. 3
c. 4
d. 5

The answer is choice B, 3. Although the first three numbers seem to be decreasing by one each position, the fourth number restarts the process. Thus, the numbers are repeating. The number after 4 will be 3.

Similar Words

In this type of problem, you will be given a set of words, three of which are similar. The question will ask you to find which word is different from the others. The key to these problems is to check for commonalities between the words and pick the word that doesn't fit.

Three of the following words are similar, while one is different. Select the one that is different.

a. Bike
b. Scooter
c. Flying
d. Skateboard

The answer is choice C, flying. Although all words have to do with transportation, flying is the only word which isn't a vehicle.

Practice Test #1

Clarity

Instructions: In the following pairs of sentences, identify the sentence that is most clearly written. If sentence "a" is clearer than sentence "b," mark "a" on your answer sheet. If sentence "b" is clearer than sentence "a," mark "b" on your answer sheet.

1.

a. The recidivism rate for older criminals was much higher than for younger criminals.
b. The recidivism rate for older criminals was much higher than younger.

2.

a. Denise remembered with a start. That she had forgotten to lock the car.
b. Denise remembered with a start that she had forgotten to lock the car.

3.

a. The officers were involved in bringing the case to a successful conclusion.
b. The officers brought the case to a successful conclusion.

4.

a. Officers and civilians occasionally come into conflict with one another; this could be avoided if they talked to them more.
b. Officers and civilians occasionally come into conflict with one another; this could be avoided if officers talked to civilians more.

5.

a. At the age of seventeen, Dave's teacher told him that he should consider medical school.
b. When Dave was seventeen, his teacher told him that he should consider medical school.

6.

a. Every February he did the same thing: renewed his library card.
b. Every February he did the same thing, renewed his library card.

7.

a. Leaders should get used to being criticized when they are wrong and ignored when they are right.
b. A leader should get used to being criticized when they are wrong and ignored when they are right.

8.

a. Throughout the interrogation, Calvin denied that the assailant was he.
b. Calvin denied throughout the interrogation that he was the assailant.

9.

a. Living near a power station can be unhealthy; it is associated with higher rates of cancer.
b. Living near a power substation can be unhealthy, it is associated with higher rates of cancer.

10.

a. Being a police officer involves a great deal of lifting weights and paperwork.
b. Being a police officer involves a great deal of lifting weights and filling out paperwork.

11.

a. You need to have a driver's license, a second form of identification, and a signed waiver to enter.
b. One needs a driver's license and a second form of identification to enter, and you have to sign a waiver as well.

12.

a. The house, which was set at the back of the property, had a number of outbuildings, including a shed.
b. The house which was set at the back of the property had a number of outbuildings including a shed.

13.

a. After reading the manual again, the inner workings of the engine made much more sense to Linda.
b. The inner workings of the engine made much more sense to Linda after she read the manual again.

14.

a. Dr. Gerard worked at the precinct station as a staff psychologist.
b. Dr. Gerard was employed at the precinct station working as a staff psychologist.

15.

a. When entering the house, the smell of almonds aroused Kevin's suspicion.
b. Kevin's suspicion was aroused by the smell of almonds as he entered the house.

16.

a. The officer pursued the suspect on foot, but he was too fast.
b. The officer pursued the suspect on foot, but the suspect was too fast.

17.

a. Community policing led to a decrease in crime over the next decade.
b. Over the next decade, community policing led to a decrease in crime.

18.

a. Many suspects will hide somewhere they are familiar with, so it is important to canvass their neighborhoods.
b. Many suspects will hide somewhere they are familiar with; so, it is important to canvass their neighborhoods.

Spelling

Instructions: In the following sentences, choose the correct spelling of the missing word.

19. "That is your fifth _______ this month," the teacher remarked sternly.

a. abscence
b. absence
c. abscess
d. absense

20. By the time the clock chimed for the _______ time, Peter was already up the stairs and in his room.

a. twelth
b. twelfth
c. twelf
d. twelvth

21. Whenever she was in that part of town, she liked to stop by and visit the _______ where her mother was buried.

a. cematery
b. cematary
c. semetary
d. cemetery

22. His soothing words and manner were able to calm even the most _______ dog.

a. vishus
b. vicous
c. viciouss
d. vicious

23. No matter how hard he tried; he could never master the _______ of the difficult piano composition.

a. rithm
b. rhythm
c. rhthm
d. rythm

24. Denise spent her Saturday mornings picking up garbage, clothes, and other _______ debris that collected along the shore by her house.

a. misselaneous
b. miscellaneous
c. miselanious
d. misselanneous

25. An effective public servant must always be _______ of the needs and desires of the community.

a. conscious
b. conchess
c. consious
d. conscience

26. The car dealership was giving away _______ replicas of its most popular sports car as a sales promotion.

a. minature
b. minercher
c. miniature
d. minacher

27. Leonard reminded the hotel clerk that he would need a _______ for his expense account.

a. reseet
b. reseat
c. receipt
d. receit

28. The court gave permission for the state to _______ all of Mr. Davis' assets after his felony conviction.

a. seize
b. seez
c. cease
d. seaz

29. The cafe's employees were instructed that hand washing should _______ any contact with food or areas where food would be prepared.

a. proceed
b. precede
c. preceed
d. preseed

30. Sloan locked her car door more frequently after hearing that there was a _______ in the neighborhood.

a. berglur
b. burglur
c. burglar
d. burgler

31. Felicia attributed the _______ noise she had heard in the night to a fight between the neighborhood cats.

a. weird
b. weerd
c. wierd
d. weyrd

32. Fred hoped he could one day be promoted all the way to _______, just as his father and grandfather had before him.

a. sergeant
b. sargent
c. sergent
d. sargeant

33. Not every state facility is able to provide _______ accommodations for males and females.

a. seperate
b. separate
c. saparate
d. sepperate

34. The lawyer has always felt _______ about protecting the rights of others.

a. passionite
b. passionate
c. passianate
d. passionet

35. Victims of crimes may be entitled to _______.

a. compensasion
b. campensation
c. compensation
d. campensasion

36. The department had several events planned on the social _______.

a. calendar
b. calender
c. calandar
d. calander

Vocabulary

Instructions: In each of the following sentences, choose the word or phrase that most nearly has the same meaning as the underlined word.

37. Only his tenacious grip enabled him to hang onto the sheer cliff face.

a. Lively
b. Fragile
c. Persistent
d. Complicated

38. The story seemed credible, but the investigators still needed to follow up on it.

a. Amazing
b. Believable
c. Dirty
d. Crumbly

39. Only the most partisan supporters of the team believed the coach's story.

a. Ignorant
b. Uninterested
c. Festive
d. Loyal

40. The premise of the movie was that time travel had become common and affordable.

a. Argument
b. Conclusion
c. Decision
d. Thought

41. A police officer who excels at her job may receive an accolade from the local media.

a. Drama
b. Compliment
c. Feature
d. Deadline

42. He seemed to be in perpetual motion without ever getting anything done.

a. Timed
b. Mobile
c. Continuous
d. Inconstant

43. An administrative oversight made it necessary for him to rescind the original oversight.

a. Invalidate
b. Put back
c. Create
d. Allege

44. He installed a solar panel so that he could generate some of his own electricity.

a. Annoy
b. Select
c. Enjoy
d. Produce

45. Sometimes even the most incompatible partners can complete some excellent work.

a. Agreeable
b. Conflicting
c. Friendly
d. Compliant

46. His material prosperity did not compensate for the personal losses he had suffered.

a. Penury
b. Possibility
c. Wealth
d. Deadliness

47. Gina was a novice but she still performed rather well.

a. Newcomer
b. Veteran
c. Senior
d. Speculator

48. He spoke with candor despite his love for the men.

a. Relevance
b. Frankness
c. Strategy
d. Gratitude

49. He tried to be prudent with his money, but he still ended up broke at the end of every month.

a. Aware
b. Calm
c. Standard
d. Cautious

50. Since Fred was young, he had had an innate ability to make other people feel comfortable.

a. Inherent
b. Intense
c. Slick
d. Prepared

51. His parents had taught him to act <u>submissive</u> and calm if he ever encountered a bear in the woods.

a. Creative
b. Passive
c. Underwater
d. Aggressive

52. The officer was unable to <u>access</u> the arrest records remotely and had to go into the office.

a. Purchase
b. Peruse
c. Obtain
d. Closer

53. Some substances sold in the drug market are heavily <u>regulated</u> by the FDA and are hard to purchase legally.

a. Shown
b. Controlled
c. Debated
d. Taxed

54. The suspect was able to <u>fashion</u> a makeshift weapon while in custody.

a. Steal
b. Manage
c. Contain
d. Construct

Reading Comprehension

Refer to the following for questions 55–56:

Randy Barron was excited to apply for a marriage license in Washington County, but he was soon met with obstacles. After Mr. Barron got through the front door of the county building, he found that the ramp going down to the Recorder of Deeds office was too steep for him to safely use his wheelchair. Additionally, there was insufficient room for him to maneuver his wheelchair to a flat surface to reach the door to the office. Barriers to accessibility mean that people like Mr. Barron will not be able to fully benefit from services and programs, including experiencing the happiest of moments of our lives, like applying for a marriage license.

55. Based on the preceding passage, which of the following statements is most accurate?

a. Randy Barron could not fit his wheelchair through the front door of the county building.
b. The door to the county building was locked, so Randy Barron could not enter.
c. Randy Barron could not navigate his wheelchair down a steep ramp.
d. Randy Barron could not push his wheelchair up a steep ramp.

56. Based on the preceding passage, which of the following statements is most accurate?

a. Randy Barron's acquisition of a marriage license was made more difficult by barriers to accessibility.
b. Randy Barron could not get married because of barriers to accessibility.
c. Handicapped people cannot get married in Washington County.
d. The Recorder of Deeds should switch offices with another county employee.

Refer to the following for questions 57–58:

When 911 or other call takers receive a request for service that they suspect involves a person with a mental illness, they should gather descriptive information on the person's behavior; determine whether the individual appears to pose a danger to himself, herself, or others; ascertain whether the person possesses or has access to weapons; and ask the caller about the person's history of mental health or substance abuse treatment, violence, or victimization. All call takers should receive training on how to collect the most useful information quickly. To supplement this training, members of the coordinating group with mental health backgrounds should develop a concise list of questions for call takers to have on hand when answering service requests that seem to involve someone with a mental illness.

57. Based on the preceding passage, which of the following statements is most accurate?

a. A 911 dispatcher is not allowed to inquire about a person's history of mental illness.
b. The mentally ill should receive the same treatment as everyone else from 911 dispatchers.
c. The list of questions for cases involving mental illness should be drafted with input from call takers.
d. There are special concerns for a 911 dispatcher when dealing with the mentally ill.

58. Based on the preceding passage, which of the following statements is most accurate?

a. A 911 operator usually gets a second chance to acquire key information.
b. It is important for 911 dispatchers to collect information quickly.
c. The mentally ill have the same access to weapons as other citizens.
d. Not every 911 call taker needs to receive training for dealing with the mentally ill.

Refer to the following for questions 59–60:

Police officers sometimes need to control violent, combative people. Their actions under such circumstances are governed by use-of-force protocols. Less-lethal technologies give police an alternative to using other physical force options that potentially are more dangerous to officers and suspects. The technologies currently in use include conducted-energy devices (such as Tasers), beanbag rounds, pepper spray, and stun grenades. When deciding to use less-lethal equipment, officers consider the circumstances and their agency's policy. Almost all larger law enforcement agencies have written policies about the use of less-lethal force. As part of their policy, agencies often have an approved use-of-force continuum to help officers decide the suitable amount of force for a situation—higher levels of force in the most severe circumstances, and less force in other circumstances. Many agencies in which officers use less-lethal technologies have training programs to help evaluate dangerous circumstances.

59. Based on the preceding passage, which of the following statements is most accurate?

a. Only a few large law enforcement agencies have written policies about the use of less-lethal force.
b. The use of less-lethal technologies reduces the danger for officers.
c. Officers are typically required to use the maximum amount of force whenever possible.
d. Stun grenades are not considered a less-lethal technology.

60. Based on the preceding passage, which of the following statements is most accurate?

a. Less-lethal technology is appropriate for any situation.
b. Officers must use their own judgment when assessing danger.
c. Less-lethal technology is an alternative to rather than a replacement for traditional physical force methods.
d. Stun grenades are an example of a conducted-energy device.

Refer to the following for questions 61–62:

Radio code is the coding system for identifying units both inside and outside the department. There are three components to every radio code. Each of these components must be included when officers are dispatched. In this coding system, units are identified with three characters: a letter designating the shift, a number designating the operational assignment, and a number identifying the area.

Shift	***Operational assignment***	***Area***
A: Day	1: Traffic division, motorcycle	1–9: North side
B: Swing	2: Traffic division, horse	10–15: East side
C: Graveyard	3: Traffic division, bicycle	16–22: West side
	4: Patrol division, platoon 1	23–29: South side
	5: Patrol division, platoon 2	30–34: Downtown
	6: Investigation division, drugs	
	7: Investigation division, financial crime	
	8: Investigation division, homicide	
	9: Administration division	

61. Using the above coding system, the call number A-3-8 would identify:

a. Day; traffic division, bicycle; north side
b. Swing; traffic division, horse; west side
c. Swing; investigation division, financial crime; east side
d. Graveyard; traffic division, horse; downtown

62. Using the above coding system, the call number C-4-33 would identify:

a. Day; patrol division, platoon 1; south side
b. Graveyard; traffic division, bicycle; west side
c. Graveyard; patrol division, platoon 1; downtown
d. Swing; traffic division, horse; south side

Refer to the following for questions 63–64:

Visibility is essential to roadside safety for emergency responders. Can drivers see and recognize an emergency vehicle as it navigates through traffic on its way to the scene of an accident or fire? When the first responder has reached the scene and is on the side of the road, can drivers clearly see both the person and the vehicle?

Several factors affect a vehicle's visibility—its size and color, for example. Environmental conditions, such as the weather and time of day, also play a role in whether drivers can easily see emergency vehicles along the road.

Emergency vehicles have features designed to draw attention to their presence even when drivers are not actively looking for them. These include warning lights, sirens and horns, and retro-reflective striping, which reflects light back to its source. Such features provide information about the vehicle's size, position, speed, and direction of travel so drivers can take suitable action.

63. Based on the preceding passage, which of the following statements is most accurate?

a. It is more important for an emergency vehicle to be visible when it is in motion.
b. Emergency vehicle sirens help improve their visibility.
c. The weather and the time of day are the only environmental conditions that affect a vehicle's visibility.
d. Emergency vehicles are always painted in special colors to improve their visibility.

64. Based on the preceding passage, which of the following statements is most accurate?

a. Emergency responders must be visible when in motion and when stopped.
b. Only emergency vehicles have features that provide information to other drivers.
c. Retro-reflective lighting is useless during the day.
d. Other drivers only need to know the location of an emergency responder in order to respond correctly.

Refer to the following for question 65:

As a Buffalo, NY parking meter mechanic, James Bagarozzo was supposed to service and repair the city's 1,200 mechanical machines, but he didn't have access to their coin canisters and was not authorized to collect money. Instead, he rigged the meters so that deposited quarters never dropped into the coin canisters. Then he retrieved the money for himself. Beginning in 2003 and continuing until the time of his arrest years later, the 57-year-old stole thousands upon thousands of quarters, using bags in his car or his deep-pocketed work pants to transfer the loot to his home, where he rolled the change in coin wrappers and exchanged it for cash at the bank.

65. Based on the preceding passage, which of the following statements is most accurate?

a. James Bagarozzo was responsible for collecting the money from parking meters in Buffalo.
b. James Bagarozzo had a criminal history before he began working as a parking meter mechanic.
c. James Bagarozzo deposited the stolen money into his bank account.
d. In Buffalo, parking meter mechanics do not have access to the coin canisters.

Refer to the following for questions 66–67:

In a sample of police departments surveyed in 2013, approximately 75% of them reported that they did not use body-worn cameras. A report about the survey notes a number of perceived benefits for using body-worn cameras, including better evidence documentation and increased accountability and transparency. But the report also notes many other factors that law enforcement executives must consider, such as privacy issues, officer and community concerns, data retention and public disclosure policies, and financial considerations. The costs of implementing body-worn cameras include not only the cost of the cameras, but also of any ancillary equipment (e.g., tablets that let officers tag data in the field), data storage and management, training, administration, and disclosure. To date, little research is available to help law enforcement executives decide whether and how to implement the use of body-worn cameras in their departments.

66. Based on the preceding passage, which of the following statements is most accurate?

a. Most police departments do not use body-worn cameras.
b. There are no disadvantages to the use of body-worn cameras.
c. Body-worn cameras are inexpensive.
d. Body-worn cameras make police officers transparent.

67. Based on the preceding passage, which of the following statements is most accurate?

a. Body-worn cameras are not right for every police department.
b. There is a large body of research on the use of body-worn cameras.
c. Most police officers prefer not to wear cameras.
d. Body-worn cameras are difficult to operate.

Refer to the following for questions 68–69:

Fire and arson investigators examine the physical attributes of a fire scene and identify and collect physical evidence from the scene. This evidence is then analyzed to help determine if the cause of the fire was accidental or deliberate. During the scene examination, investigators may find evidence such as accelerants, tampered utilities, and specific burn patterns, which may indicate criminal activity.

68. Based on the preceding passage, which of the following statements is most accurate?

a. Burn patterns indicate criminal activity.
b. Arson investigators do not always find evidence of criminal activity at a fire scene.
c. Arson investigators question suspects and try to establish motive.
d. Arson investigators are responsible for analyzing the physical evidence collected at the scene.

69. Based on the preceding passage, which of the following best represents the order of events in a fire investigation?

a. Arrive on the scene, collect relevant evidence, analyze the evidence.
b. Analyze the burn patterns, identify other evidence, collect all evidence for further analysis.
c. Create a hypothesis on whether the fire was intentional, collect all evidence, analyze evidence to prove or disprove the hypothesis.
d. Make a list of suspects, collect relevant evidence, analyze the evidence.

Refer to the following for question 70:

Suspects in cars who flee from law enforcement place themselves, the officers, and bystanders in hazardous situations. High-speed pursuits often result in property damage and may result in injury or death. About half of all high-speed pursuits last less than two minutes and most last less than six minutes. Officers must act instantly, weighing the need to protect public safety against the need to apprehend fleeing suspects.

70. Based on the preceding passage, which of the following statements is most accurate?

a. High-speed pursuits cause more injuries than deaths.
b. High-speed pursuits require officers to make the right decision in an instant.
c. Most high-speed pursuits are longer than six minutes.
d. High-speed pursuits are the largest cause of officer fatalities.

Refer to the following for question 71:

Law enforcement officers often use conducted-energy devices (CEDs) to get noncompliant or hostile suspects to comply. CEDs, such as Tasers, induce involuntary muscle contractions, causing the suspect to be temporarily incapacitated. CEDs are controversial because of safety concerns. The concerns are not solely with the technology itself but with the policies and training for using the devices. Clearly defined policies and thorough training are needed to ensure that any use-of-force technique is used only when necessary to protect officers, suspects, and bystanders. When CEDs are properly used as an alternative to deadly force, they can help reduce injuries to officers and suspects alike.

71. Based on the preceding passage, which of the following statements is most accurate?

a. CEDs are a totally safe alternative to conventional methods of force.
b. CEDs are not totally safe, but they are safer than conventional methods of force.
c. Most police departments provide extensive training related to the use of conducted-energy devices.
d. Tasers are not an example of a conducted-energy device.

Refer to the following for questions 72–73:

There is a specific protocol for classifying crimes, and law enforcement officers are required to follow this protocol at all times. Victimizations and incidents are classified based on detailed characteristics of the event provided by the respondent. Neither victims nor interviewers classify crimes at the time of interview. During data processing, a computer program classifies each event into one type of crime, based on the entries on a number of items on the survey questionnaire. This ensures that similar events will be classified using a standard procedure. The glossary definition for each crime indicates the major characteristics required to be so classified. If an event can be classified as more than one type of crime, a hierarchy is used that classifies the crime according to the most serious event that occurred. The hierarchy is: rape, sexual assault, robbery, assault, burglary, motor vehicle theft, theft.

72. Based on the preceding passage, which of the following statements is most accurate?

a. Crimes are not classified while victims are being interviewed.
b. The crime classification system only needs to be observed occasionally.
c. Crime classification is based on the first offense reported by the victim.
d. Police officers have control over the items on the survey questionnaire.

73. Based on the preceding passage, which of the following statements is most accurate?

a. Theft is a more serious crime than robbery.
b. Motor vehicle theft is a more serious crime than assault.
c. Sexual assault is a more serious crime than motor vehicle theft.
d. Assault is a more serious crime than robbery.

Refer to the following for questions 74–75:

There are some easy ways for employers to reduce employee theft. Employees who are treated fairly and generously are less likely to steal. Get to know your employees. Ask for their suggestions and seriously consider them. Involve employees in crime prevention practices. Consider starting a profit-sharing program. Make sure your salary rates are competitive—an underpaid employee may feel that stealing from you merely "makes up the difference."

74. Based on the preceding passage, which of the following statements is most accurate?

a. Strong relationships between owners and employees decrease the incidence of employee theft.
b. Employees at thriving businesses are less likely to steal.
c. Employees should lead crime prevention practices.
d. Employee theft can be reduced by encouraging competition between employees.

75. Based on the preceding passage, which of the following statements is most accurate?

a. Sometimes employees steal because they feel that they are underpaid.
b. Employees should be paid as much as their employers.
c. Businesses with profit-sharing programs always experience less employee theft.
d. Employee theft is the most common crime in the workplace.

Refer to the following for questions 76–77:

Well-trained K9s play a vital role in many police forces. Some assist their handlers in scent-focused tasks, like narcotic and explosive device detection and tracking suspects or missing persons. Others are trained to respond with aggression on command, attacking a suspect and detaining them when an officer is unable to do so. Thanks to their speed, smelling abilities, and intelligence, German Shepherds, Labrador Retrievers, and Belgian Malinois are the most popular dogs used in law enforcement. The style and length of training required by these dogs is dependent on their intended use. Following initial training, dogs are assigned to officers who act as their handlers. Handlers are responsible for the daily care and training of their K9s, including regular practice of their skills to keep them at the top of their game.

76. Based on the preceding passage, which of the following statements is most accurate?

a. Police dogs are a necessary part of the success of all police forces.
b. Once trained, police dogs will work until retirement with no additional training needed.
c. Police dogs can perform a variety of tasks for their handlers.
d. Only German Shepherds, Labrador Retrievers, and Belgian Malinois are able to become K9 officers.

77. Based on the preceding passage, which of the following statements is most accurate?

a. Many police dogs live at the station full time.
b. Some police dogs can be used to detect drugs in a suspect's vehicle.
c. A police dog can have false alerts.
d. It is necessary that a K9 be specialized in one task.

Refer to the following for questions 78–79:

Every year, there are more than 10 million cases of domestic violence that require the attention of law enforcement. Domestic violence is any type of abusive behavior used to gain or maintain power over a partner or other member of the household. Swift and careful response is key to maintaining the safety of all parties involved when responding to a domestic violence call. Officers should use their discretion in responding to calls and determine if the use of sirens while responding may alert the offender to stop confrontation before authorities can bear witness or if it may further increase the offender's aggression. Separating the abuser from the victim or victims when obtaining statements helps ensure safety and increases the chance of truthful statements. When possible, two officers should respond to these calls, as opposed to only one, to help make this possible. In all cases, thorough evidence must be collected and documented in writing. These documents help track repeat offenders. Arrests must be made in situations where officers have probable cause to believe that an offense has taken place or where a protection order has been violated. In instances where arrests are not made, responding officers should include detailed explanations as to why that was the case in their reports.

78. Based on the preceding passage, which of the following statements is most accurate?

a. Arrests must be made following all responses to domestic violence calls.
b. Officers must respond to domestic violence calls in the same manner they respond to other calls.
c. Domestic violence calls make up the majority of calls received at US police departments.
d. It is necessary for officers to write detailed reports following responses to domestic violence calls.

79. Based on the preceding passage, which of the following statements is most accurate?

a. Domestic violence is committed as an act of power.
b. Domestic violence is a leading cause of arrests.
c. Domestic violence calls are usually over quickly.
d. Domestic violence is a gateway crime.

Refer to the following for questions 80–81:

School shooting incidents in the US are steadily rising. In order to be prepared to respond efficiently, local police departments should develop tactical plans for the schools in their jurisdictions. A site survey should be conducted to allow officers to assess the school's floor plan, locate entries, determine areas for command and staging, locate utility cutoffs, and identify any safety risks that need to be corrected. A secondary, off-campus location where students and staff can be moved if needed should also be identified. Plans to control traffic flow should be considered, as many parents, guardians, and media representatives will likely begin arriving on the scene almost as quickly as officers. It may be necessary to block off surrounding streets for safety. Collectively, this information is used to devise a tactical response plan. By taking the time to be proactive and determine the initial course of action police will take when responding to an active school shooting, officers will be able to neutralize the shooter quickly. This will lead to fewer casualties and quicker aid for victims.

80. Based on the preceding passage, which of the following statements is most accurate?

a. Traffic to the area should be controlled before a shooter is neutralized.
b. A quick, effective response to school shootings by authorities will lead to fewer deaths.
c. Creating a tactical plan is the responsibility of school district officials.
d. Being proactive in creating a plan will deter school shooters.

81. Based on the preceding passage, which of the following statements is most accurate?

a. Plans to control media representatives are a critical component of tactical plans.
b. Having a secondary location to move students to is only necessary if the school needs to close portions of its campus.
c. Site surveys are a necessary part of developing a comprehensive plan for responding to a school shooting.
d. Students play a large role in the development of the department's tactical plan.

Refer to the following for question 82:

When searching for a suspect that has fled in an identified vehicle, officers can use Automated License Plate Readers (ALPR) to help find them. ALPRs take photos of vehicles and their license plates. Optical character recognition is used to turn the letters and numbers in the photograph into an alphanumeric sequence that can be compared to multiple databases containing license plate information on wanted vehicles. If a match is found, authorities are alerted. In some cases, ALPRs help find perpetrators by providing license plates for cars in the area that match a description of vehicles used in crimes. Officers can use this information to determine who the vehicle belongs to. ALPRs can be mounted to poles, signs, stoplights, or police cars. They scan all passing vehicles.

82. Based on the preceding passage, which of the following statements is most accurate?

a. ALPRs are only helpful if officers know the license plate of the vehicle they are looking for.
b. ALPRs only photograph cars that match the descriptions of wanted vehicles.
c. Officers must manually check ALPR lists to find matches of wanted vehicles.
d. ALPRs compare the collected information to lists of wanted vehicles.

Cloze

It (83) ____ a great deal of time and effort, but the Davis County Police Department (84) ___ eventually able to catch a sophisticated jewel thief who had been breaking (85) ____ expensive homes for at least two years. The evidence gathered (86) ____ the criminal's hideout suggested that at least 50 homes in the area had (87) ____ burglarized.

The burglaries began in March of 2008, (88) ____ an elderly woman in the exclusive Haverford Heights subdivision reported that (89) __ antique pearl necklace had (90) ____ stolen from her dresser while she was out of town. The evidence found (91) __ the woman's home would become very familiar to the detectives who worked on (92) ____ case: a bathroom window had been forced (93) ____ with a crowbar, and someone had crawled in. There (94) ____ footprints in the dirt outside the window, but police found the shoes that made the (95) ______ in a garbage can down the street. This (96) ___ a trademark of the burglar: he or she always wore new (97) _____, which were discarded immediately (98) _____ the job was finished.

After the first burglary, (99) _____ was a short period in which the criminal was inactive. However, two months later, he (100) __ she struck again. A set of diamond earrings was stolen (101) ____ the home of a vacationing couple, (102) ___ several precious stones were taken from an elderly woman. Each time, the (103) ______ found a pair of new shoes in a nearby garbage can. Within the department, the detectives began referring to the (104) _____ as "the Size Eleven Bandit." However, despite their best efforts, they could (105) ___ make a break in the case.

The burglaries then increased in frequency, (106) ____ seven occurring over the next three months. The police (107) _____ tell that the criminal was becoming more brazen, but they still were unable to make any headway in the case. It was clear that the criminal was intelligent and patient, and (108) ____ a great deal about precious stones. However, he or she was (109) ____ very careful to avoid leaving behind any clues that would (110) ____ the detectives.

The burglaries continued for more than a year. Several times, the police (111) ____ sure that they had made a break in the case, but each of these leads dried up in the end. Finally, one of the detectives working on the case assembled a (112) ____ of all the shoes found at the various crime scenes and took this list around to all of the shoe stores (113) __ the area. It turned out that only one (114) _____ sold all of the different types of shoes worn (115) __ the burglar during his or her crimes. The detective then examined the sales records of the store and discovered (116) ____ several of the shoes had been purchased (117) ____ the same credit card, a (118) ____ belonging to Kevin Fuller of Finley Station. A (119) ______ of Fuller's home revealed a stash of stolen jewelry, and Fuller himself (120) ___ apprehended later that week as (121) __ shopped for groceries. He immediately confessed (122) __ the burglaries.

Reasoning

Instructions: Officers often face situations in which they need to determine how different pieces of information relate to one another. In this section, you will be presented with information such as a group or ordered series of facts, numbers, letters, or words. Your task is to study the various pieces of information and try to understand how they relate to one another.

123. Identify the next number in the series: 45, 42, 39, 36, 33...

a. 29
b. 35
c. 32
d. 30

124. In the three-legged race, Aaron finished after Bruce, but before Carl. In what order did the participants finish?

a. Carl, Aaron, Bruce
b. Aaron, Carl, Bruce
c. Bruce, Aaron, Carl
d. Carl, Bruce, Aaron

125. Three of the following words are similar, while one is different. Select the one that is different.

a. Ramp
b. House
c. Castle
d. Shack

126. Identify the next number in the series: 12, 27, 36, 12, 27, 36, 12...

a. 12
b. 27
c. 36
d. 49

127. Ellen, Fiona, Gretchen, and Helen were in a race. Ellen finished ahead of Gretchen, and the other two girls tied. Who came in second place?

a. Ellen
b. Gretchen
c. Helen
d. Not enough information

128. On their last Spanish test, Dave received a 92 and scored ten points better than Edgar. However, Edgar scored four points better than Philip, who scored three points better than Quincy. What was Philip's score?

a. 75
b. 78
c. 82
d. 85

129. Identify the next number in the series: 1, 2, 5, 10, 17, 26...

a. 35
b. 37
c. 38
d. 40

130. Frank weighs more than George, and George weighs less than Henry. Who weighs the most?

a. Frank
b. George
c. Henry
d. Not enough information

131. Three of the following words are similar, while one is different. Select the one that is different.

a. Fierce
b. Container
c. Quiet
d. Grainy

Answer Key and Explanations for Test #1

Clarity

1. A: In the incorrect version of the sentence, the comparison being made is not clear. The correct version of the sentence makes it clear that the comparison is with younger criminals and not just younger people in general. Including the word *criminal* at the end of the sentence makes the comparison clear.

2. B: The incorrect answer consists of a sentence and a sentence fragment. The expression "That she had forgotten to lock the car" is a subordinate clause and cannot stand alone as a sentence. Indeed, this clause is essential to the preceding sentence, because it indicates what Denise remembered. The correct answer contains all of the relevant information and is the best choice.

3. B: The alternative version is too wordy. It is unnecessary to say "were involved in bringing" when the same meaning can be conveyed by "brought." In writing, it is best to use the minimum number of words necessary.

4. B: In the incorrect version of the sentence, it is not totally clear what *they* and *them* refer to in the second clause. The reader may not be able to tell whether the officers or the civilians should be talking to the other more.

5. B: In the other version of the sentence, the subject of the introductory clause is unclear. It is not apparent whether Dave or his teacher was seventeen when Dave's teacher told him to consider medical school. Of course, the reader probably will guess that the writer meant to say that Dave was seventeen, but this guesswork should not be required of a reader. The correct version of the sentence makes it plain that the event in question occurred when Dave was seventeen.

6. A: The other version would be considered a run-on sentence because there is no conjunction (*like*, *and*, or *but*) after the comma. The correct version of the sentence uses a colon, a mark of punctuation that can function in much the same way as a conjunction. In this case, it introduces the answer to the question posed by the first part of the sentence.

7. A: In the other version of the sentence, the subject is singular but the subsequent pronouns are plural. It is common for them to be used this way, but it is ungrammatical and potentially confusing for the reader. In the correct version of the sentence, the subject has been made plural to agree with the pronouns.

8. B: The other version is awkward and incorrectly uses the subject pronoun *he* at the end when it should use the object pronoun *him*. Rephrasing the sentence to eliminate the introductory clause makes it much easier to read, and restructuring the end of the sentence fixes the pronoun error.

9. A: The other version is a run-on sentence, in which two independent clauses are not connected properly. Because the second clause clarifies the first, it is appropriate to separate them with a semicolon.

10. B: When a sentence contains a list (in this case, a list of the things a police officer does a great deal of), the items in the list should be expressed in the same grammatical terms. Because "lifting weights" includes a verb, every other item in the list should include a verb as well. In the incorrect version of the sentence, it sounds as if a police officer must lift paperwork and weights. There are other correct ways that this sentence could be written, for instance, "Being a police officer involves a great deal of weights and paperwork." In this version, none of the items in the list are accompanied by a verb. The important thing is for the treatment of list items to be consistent. In grammar, this is known as parallel structure.

11. A: The incorrect sentence has two different subjects: *one* in the first clause and *you* in the second. Although the reader would probably be able to make sense of this sentence, it is unnecessarily confusing. In the correct version of the sentence, there is a single subject.

12. A: Commas are necessary to set off the two subordinate clauses, "which was set at the back of the property" and "including a shed." The sentence becomes much easier to read when the commas are added, because the reader is encouraged to take the appropriate pauses.

13. B: In the other version of the sentence, the initial clause does not indicate who read the manual. The reader will probably guess that Linda was the reader, but it is also possible that there was some other, unnamed manual reader. The incorrect version of the sentence is needlessly confusing.

14. A: The other version of the sentence is redundant. There is no need to say both "was employed" and "worked." The correct version of the sentence eliminates one of these phrases and makes the sentence easier to read. It would also be correct to write, "Dr. Gerard was employed at the precinct station as a staff psychologist."

15. B: The other version of the sentence has a confusing introductory clause. The wording of that version creates the impression that the smell of almonds, rather than Kevin, was entering the house.

16. B: In sentence A, it is not clear who is too fast. The "he" in the sentence could be referring to the officer or the suspect. The correct version of the sentence clarifies that the suspect was too fast.

17. A: Both sentences include the same information and are grammatically correct. Sentence A uses a more direct grammatical structure that places the emphasis on the subject and action of "community policing." Sentence B places a stronger emphasis on the timeline, "over the next decade." This may be appropriate in a specific context, but as an isolated sentence, it feels unnecessarily passive.

18. A: A semicolon is used to separate independent clauses that are not joined by a coordinating conjunction like *so*. Since both sentences join independent clauses with a coordinating conjunction, a semicolon is incorrect here.

Spelling

19. B: absence

20. B: twelfth

21. D: cemetery

22. D: vicious

23. B: rhythm

24. B: miscellaneous

25. A: conscious

26. C: miniature

27. C: receipt

28. A: seize

29. B: precede

30. C: burglar

31. A: weird

32. A: sergeant

33. B: separate

34. B: passionate

35. C: compensation

36. A: calendar

Vocabulary

37. C: *Persistent* most nearly has the same meaning as *tenacious.* Both of them refer to the quality of never giving up, or continuing to attempt something no matter the resistance or the result.

38. B: *Believable* most nearly has the same meaning as *credible.* Both of these words mean easy to agree with or believe.

39. D: *Loyal* most nearly has the same meaning as *partisan.* Both of these words refer to people who endorse and contribute to the success of a particular cause.

40. A: *Argument* most nearly has the same meaning as *premise.* Both of them refer to an idea or concept that is being advanced.

41. B: *Compliment* most nearly has the same meaning as *accolade.* Both of them are nouns that mean praise or positive words.

42. C: *Continuous* most nearly has the same meaning as *perpetual.* Both of these adjectives refer to things that never stop or are ongoing.

43. A: *Invalidate* most nearly has the same meaning as *rescind.* Both of these verbs mean to declare something null and void.

44. D: *Produce* most nearly has the same meaning as *generate.* These verbs mean to make or create.

45. B: *Conflicting* most nearly has the same meaning as *incompatible.* Both of these adjectives refer to people or things that disagree, do not get along, or do not go well together.

46. C: *Wealth* most nearly has the same meaning as *prosperity.* Both of them refer to affluence or an abundance of riches.

47. A: *Newcomer* most nearly has the same meaning as *novice*. Both refer to a person who is new or is just beginning to learn something.

48. B: *Frankness* most nearly has the same meaning as *candor*. Both of these nouns mean total honesty, even when what is being expressed is unpopular or unpleasant.

49. D: *Cautious* most nearly has the same meaning as *prudent*. Both of these words mean careful and safe.

50. A: *Inherent* most nearly has the same meaning as *innate*. Both of these adjectives mean built-in or ingrained.

51. B: *Passive* most nearly has the same meaning as *submissive*. These words refer to people who are not in charge and do not attempt to be in control.

52. C: *Obtain* has the closest meaning to *access*. In the context of this sentence, both of these words mean "to acquire" the records.

53. B: *Controlled* has the closest meaning to *regulated*. Both words mean "to heavily supervise by a set of rules."

54. D: *Construct* has the closest meaning to *fashion*. In the context of this sentence, both words mean "to build or create something."

Reading Comprehension

55. C: Based on the passage, the most accurate statement is that Randy Barron could not navigate his wheelchair down a steep ramp. Indeed, the second sentence of the passage states that "the ramp going down to the Recorder of Deeds office was too steep for him to safely use his wheelchair." The passage does not indicate that the door to the county building was locked or too narrow, though it does state that there was not enough room for Barron to maneuver his wheelchair. The passage does not say anything about Barron having a hard time going up a ramp: the only ramp mentioned in the passage is one that Barron must go down.

56. A: Based on the passage, the most accurate statement is that Randy Barron's acquisition of a marriage license was made more difficult by barriers to accessibility. This is the main idea of the passage, which begins by describing Barron's excitement and then discusses the various problems that made his task harder. The final sentence summarizes the idea: "Barriers to accessibility mean that people...will not be able to fully benefit from services and programs." The passage never states that Barron was unable to get married at all, just that the process was more difficult than necessary. The passage never states that the door was locked or that Washington County forbids handicapped people from getting married. Finally, there is no suggestion that the Recorder of Deeds should switch offices with another county employee. This switch would do nothing to diminish the problems of the handicapped.

57. D: Based on the passage, the most accurate statement is that there are special concerns for a 911 dispatcher when dealing with the mentally ill. This statement is not made explicitly, but it is the main idea of the passage nonetheless. The passage indicates in several ways that 911 call takers should receive special training for dealing with cases involving the mentally ill. The passage does not state that a 911 dispatcher is not allowed to inquire about a person's history of mental illness: on the contrary, the first sentence states that this is one of the first inquiries the call taker should make. The passage describes the special concerns and protocol for dealing with the mentally ill, so clearly it does not state that the mentally ill should receive the same treatment as everyone else. Finally, the passage states that a list of questions should be developed by "members of the coordinating group with mental health backgrounds," not call takers.

58. B: Based on the passage, the most accurate statement is that it is important for 911 dispatchers to collect information quickly. The passages specifically states that "all call takers should receive training on how to collect the most useful information quickly." The passage does not indicate that 911 operators get more than one chance to acquire key information; on the contrary, the passage suggests that vital information must be collected as quickly as possible. The passage mentions that the call taker should inquire about the mentally ill person's access to weapons, but it does not provide any information about the amount of access given to the mentally ill relative to other citizens. Finally, the passage directly states that all 911 operators should be trained in obtaining the key information about the mentally ill.

59. B: Based on the passage, the most accurate statement is that the use of less-lethal technologies reduces the danger for officers. The third sentence of the passage states that other options "potentially are more dangerous to officers and suspects." It could be presumed that the use of more aggressive weapons leads to more instances of violent retaliation by suspects, as well as more instances in which the officer's own weaponry is turned against him or her. As for the other answer choices, the passage states directly that "almost all larger law enforcement agencies have written policies about the use of less-lethal force." Also, the passage does not indicate that officers are typically required to use the maximum amount of force whenever possible; instead, it states that officers are taught to use higher levels of force only in the most severe circumstances. Finally, stun grenades are mentioned as an example of a less-lethal technology.

60. C: Based on the passage, the most accurate statement is that less-lethal technology is an alternative to rather than a replacement for traditional physical force methods. The passage makes clear that less-lethal technology will not be suitable in all situations, and that there may be some cases in which higher levels of force are required. The assessment of danger is not entirely left to the judgment of the officer. According to the passage, "many agencies...have training programs to help evaluate dangerous circumstances." At another point, the passage describes how many large agencies have an "approved use-of-force continuum" that helps officers determine the appropriate response. Finally, the passage gives Tasers, not stun grenades, as an example of a conducted-energy device.

61. A: Using the above coding system, the call number A-3-8 would identify day; traffic division, bicycle; north side.

62. C: Using the above coding system, the call number C-4-33 would identify graveyard; patrol division, platoon 1; downtown.

63. B: Based on the passage, the most accurate statement is that emergency vehicle sirens help improve their visibility. Though this may seem counterintuitive, sirens and horns improve visibility simply by encouraging other drivers to look in the direction of the vehicle. As the passage states, these features are "designed to draw attention...even when drivers are not actively looking." The passage does not say that it is more important for an emergency vehicle to be visible when it is in motion; it implies that visibility is important both when the vehicle is in motion and when it is stopped. Next, the passage does not state that weather and time of day are the *only* environmental conditions that affect a vehicle's visibility, though these are given as examples of important environmental conditions. Furthermore, the passage never suggests that emergency vehicles are always painted in special colors to improve their visibility, though the information provided by the passage does suggest that this would be a good idea.

64. A: Based on the passage, the most accurate statement is that emergency responders must be visible when in motion and when stopped. This is made clear in the first paragraph, when the passage describes how an emergency vehicle must be seen "as it navigates through traffic" and "on the side of the road." It is not true that only emergency vehicles have features that provide information to other drivers: for one thing, all cars have warning lights that tell other cars when they are braking. The passage does not state that retro-reflective lighting is useless during the day. Finally, the passage states that other drivers need to know several factors about an emergency vehicle, including its "size, position, speed, and direction of travel" in order to respond correctly.

65. D: Based on the passage, the most accurate statement is that in Buffalo, parking meter mechanics do not have access to the coin canisters. This fact is made plain in the first sentence, where it states that James Bagarozzo (and other parking meter mechanics) "didn't have access to [the] coin canisters and was not authorized to collect money." With this in mind, it is clear that James Bagarozzo was not responsible for collecting the money from parking meters in Buffalo. There is also no indication that Bagarozzo had a criminal history before he began working as a parking meter mechanic. Finally, the passage does not suggest that Bagarozzo deposited the money into his bank account: on the contrary, it states that he took it to the bank and exchanged it for cash.

66. A: Based on the passage, the most accurate statement is that most police departments do not use body-worn cameras. The first sentence states that a recent survey found that around three-quarters of police departments do not use body-worn cameras. The passage describes the pros and cons of using these cameras, so it is inaccurate to state that there are no disadvantages to their use. Among the disadvantages is the cost of the cameras, as they are not inexpensive and require costly accessories and training. Finally, body-worn cameras do not make police officers transparent; rather, they encourage departmental transparency insofar as they make it difficult for police officers to misrepresent their actions.

67. A: Based on the passage, the most accurate statement is that body-worn cameras are not right for every police department. The passage suggests that the costs may be too high for some departments. The last sentence of the passage states that there is as yet not enough research for law enforcement executives to properly decide whether to obtain these cameras. From this last sentence, it is clear that there is not a large body of research on this technology. The passage also does not indicate whether police officers prefer to wear the cameras. Lastly, the passage does not state that the cameras are difficult to use, though it does mention that training is required.

68. B: Based on the passage, the most accurate statement is that arson investigators do not always find evidence of criminal activity at a fire scene. The last sentence states that investigators "*may* find evidence...which *may* indicate criminal activity." In other words, investigators do not always find such evidence. Similarly, the passage indicates that some burn patterns suggest criminal activity, but not that all do. The passage does not state that arson investigators question suspects and try to establish motive. Moreover, the passage does not indicate that the investigators themselves analyze the evidence, simply that the evidence is analyzed.

69. A: It is important to be able to determine a sequence of events from a passage, and sometimes that sequence is implied. While the passage never mentions investigators arriving on the scene, we can infer that, if they are inspecting the scene, they have already arrived there. Option B is incorrect because the passage uses the signal word "then" in the second sentence to indicate that evidence, such as burn patterns, is analyzed after it is collected. Options C and D are incorrect because the passage gives no indication as to when hypotheses are created or a list of suspects is generated.

70. B: Based on the passage, the most accurate statement is that high-speed pursuits require officers to make the right decision in an instant. The passage states this in the last sentence. There is no indication that high-speed pursuits cause more injuries than deaths. The passage states that most high-speed pursuits last fewer than six minutes. Finally, the passage does not assert that high-speed pursuits are the largest cause of officer fatalities, though it does indicate that these pursuits are hazardous to officers.

71. B: Based on the passage, the most accurate statement is that CEDs are not totally safe, but they are safer than conventional methods of force. This fact is made plain in the last sentence, where the author states that conducted-energy devices can reduce injuries to both officers and suspects relative to conventional methods of force.

72. A: Based on the passage, the most accurate statement is that crimes are not classified while victims are being interviewed. On the contrary, the passage states directly that "during data processing, a computer program classifies each event into one type of crime, based on the entries on a number of items on the survey questionnaire." The protocol, then, is for police to help victims fill out a survey, the results of which are used by a computer to classify the crime. The passage makes plain in the first sentence that "law enforcement are required to follow this protocol at all times," so it would be incorrect to say that it only needs to be observed occasionally. Crime classification is not based on the first offense reported by the victim, but rather on "the most serious event that occurred." Finally, the passage does not suggest that police officers have control over the items on the survey questionnaire. Though the passage does not state this directly, it implies that the survey questionnaire consists of a standard set of questions so that classification will be performed in a consistent manner.

73. C: Based on the passage, the most accurate statement is that sexual assault is a more serious crime than motor vehicle theft. This judgment is made according to the hierarchy given in the final sentence. According to this hierarchy, the most serious event is rape and the least serious event is theft.

74. A: Based on the passage, the most accurate statement is that strong relationships between owners and employees decrease the incidence of employee theft. This is indicated at several points in the passage, such as when the writer states that employers should "get to know [their] employees." The passage does not suggest that thriving businesses are less likely to have employee theft. Likewise, the passage does not state that employees should lead crime prevention practices, merely that they should be involved. Finally, the passage does not state that competition between employees will reduce employee theft, though it does argue that offering competitive salary rates will discourage theft.

75. A: Based on the passage, the most accurate statement is that sometimes employees steal because they feel that they are underpaid. The second sentence of the passage states that "employees who are treated fairly and generously are less likely to steal," and the last sentence encourages employers to "make sure [their] salary rates are competitive." Clearly, well-compensated employees will be less inclined to steal from their employers. There is no suggestion, however, that employees should be paid as much as their employers, or that employee theft is the most common crime in the workplace. Finally, though the passage does imply that profit-sharing programs can be a useful strategy for reducing employee theft, there is no assertion that these programs always are successful in doing so.

76. C: Based on the passage, the most accurate statement is that police dogs can perform a variety of tasks for their handlers. This passage explains that police K9s can perform several different scent-based tasks as well as detain suspects. While the passage opens by saying that K9s play a vital role in many police forces, it does not deem them a necessity for all forces as in choice A. There is no mention of dogs working until retirement, as choice B suggests, only that regular practice is needed to hone their skills. The passage expresses that German shepherds, Labrador retrievers, and Belgian Malinois are the top three choices for police dogs, but it does not state that they are the only options as stated in choice D.

77. B: Based on the passage, the most accurate statement is that some police dogs can be used to detect drugs in a suspect's vehicle. The passage explains that some K9s assist their handlers in scent-focused tasks like detecting narcotics, which suggests they can detect drugs. There is no mention of where police dogs live, as choice A says, just that they are the responsibility of their handlers. There is also no mention of false alerts, contrary to what choice C argues. The passage mentions several tasks a K9 officer can perform, but, unlike what is suggested in choice D, it does not state that they must be specialized in one.

78. D: Based on the passage, the most accurate statement is that it is necessary for officers to write detailed reports following responses to domestic violence calls. The passage highlights this in two ways. It states that, in all cases, thorough evidence must be collected and documented in writing. It also states that detailed reasons as to why no arrests were made must be provided if no arrests are made. Arrests are not made in all cases, contrary to what choice A says, specifically when there is no probable cause and no protection order violation. Unlike what is stated in choice B, officers should use their discretion in responding to domestic violence calls and determine if arriving with their lights and sirens on may worsen the situation. There is not enough information given to determine if the over 10 million domestic violence calls received per year make up the majority of calls in the US as choice C states.

79. A: Based on the passage, the most accurate statement is that domestic violence is committed as an act of power. The passage defines domestic violence as "any type of abusive behavior used to gain or maintain power over a partner or other member of the household." There are no statistics provided to support the statement in choice B that domestic violence is the leading cause of arrests. Choice C is not correct because no timeline of domestic violence calls is provided by the passage. Unlike what is said in choice D, the passage does not suggest or state that domestic violence is a gateway crime, which is a crime for which one faces few consequences and which leads to the offender committing more serious crimes in the future.

80. B: Based on the passage, the most accurate statement is that a quick, effective response to school shootings by authorities will lead to fewer deaths. This is explained in the passage's two final sentences. Though traffic is discussed in the passage before neutralizing the shooter is, it is not necessary to control traffic before neutralizing the shooter as is stated in choice A. Tactical plans should be created by police departments for the schools in their jurisdictions and not by school district officials as stated by choice C. Unlike what is claimed in choice D, the passage does not suggest that creating these plans will deter school shooters. Instead, they will only make the police response more efficient.

81. C: Based on the passage, the most accurate statement is that site surveys are a necessary part of developing a comprehensive plan for responding to a school shooting. The passage explains how doing so leads to a quicker response and fewer casualties. Plans to control the media are not pertinent to a tactical plan, contrary to what choice A states, outside of ensuring that members of the media do not get in the way of neutralizing the shooter. Choice B is incorrect because having a

secondary location is a necessary part of a comprehensive tactical plan, regardless of the school's need to close any part of their campus. Choice D is incorrect because students are not involved in the development of a tactical plan.

82. D: Based on the passage, the most accurate statement is that ALPRs compare the collected information to lists of wanted vehicles. The passage says that the information collected is compared to multiple databases, which would contain lists of wanted vehicles. ALPRs can help identify the owners of vehicles involved in crimes by finding vehicles that match the given description and providing their license plate information, so choice A is incorrect. ALPRs scan all vehicles that pass, as stated in the last sentence—not just cars that match the descriptions of wanted vehicles like choice B claims. Choice C is incorrect because officers do not have to manually check ALPR lists because the software compares collected information against databases and alerts officers if the vehicle they are looking for is scanned.

Cloze

83	took	**93**	open	**103**	police	**113**	in
84	was	**94**	were	**104**	thief	**114**	store
85	into	**95**	prints	**105**	not	**115**	by
86	from	**96**	was	**106**	with	**116**	that
87	been	**97**	shoes	**107**	could	**117**	with
88	when	**98**	after	**108**	knew	**118**	card
89	an	**99**	there	**109**	also	**119**	search
90	been	**100**	or	**110**	help	**120**	was
91	in or at	**101**	from	**111**	were	**121**	he
92	this	**102**	and	**112**	list	**122**	to

Reasoning

123. D: The next number in the series is 30. In this series, each successive number is three less than the number that preceded it. So, to find the next number in the series, simply subtract three from the last number given.

124. C: The correct order of finish is Bruce, Aaron, and then Carl. According to the prompt, Aaron finished after Bruce but before Carl. Bruce, therefore, must have finished before Carl as well. Since Aaron was in between the other two finishers, the order of finish must be Bruce, Aaron, and Carl.

125. A: The word *ramp* is not like the other three. A house, castle, or shack is a place where someone could live; a ramp is not.

126. B: The pattern is a recurring series of three numbers: 12, 27, and 36. Therefore, a 27 would follow the 12.

127. D: There is not enough information to solve this problem. There is no indication as to where the two girls who tied finished in relation to Ellen and Gretchen. That is, Fiona and Helen may have finished ahead of Ellen and Gretchen, in between them, or after them. Therefore, it is impossible to say who finished in second place.

128. B: Philip scored a 78. Since Edgar scored ten points worse than Dave, who got a 92, then Edgar must have gotten an 82. If Philip scored four points worse, then he got a 78.

129. B: The next number in the series is 37. In this pattern, the gap between each successive pair of numbers is 1, then 3, then 5, etc. In other words, the gap increases by two each time. Therefore, since the difference between 17 and 26 is 9, the difference between the next two numbers will be 11, and so the next number in the sequence will be 37.

130. D: There is not enough information to answer this question. It is clear that both Frank and Henry weigh more than George, but it is impossible to tell which of those two weighs more.

131. B: The word *container* is not like the other three. *Fierce, quiet,* and *grainy* are all adjectives: that is, they are words used to describe nouns or noun phrases. *Container,* on the other hand, is a noun. Nouns refer to people, places, or things.

Practice Test #2

Clarity

Instructions: In the following pairs of sentences, identify the sentence that is most clearly written. If sentence "a" is clearer than sentence "b," mark "a" on your answer sheet. If sentence "b" is clearer than sentence "a," mark "b" on your answer sheet.

1.

a. When Frank arrived at the festival, he remembered that he had left his credit card at the store and must go back to retrieve it.
b. When Frank arrived at the festival, he remembered that he had left his credit card at the store, so he had to go back to retrieve it.

2.

a. Victor, who had never been to Canada, was nonetheless accused of smuggling cigarettes over the border, which was a felony.
b. Victor who had never been to Canada was nonetheless accused of smuggling cigarettes over the border which was a felony.

3.

a. In pursuit of the suspect, he dodged trash cans, boxes, and through red lights.
b. In pursuit of the suspect, he dodged trash cans, leapt over boxes, and ran through red lights.

4.

a. He could not be held because the investigators had made several errors during the collection of evidence.
b. The reason he could not be held was because the investigators had made several errors during the collection of evidence.

5.

a. The officer courteously asked the crowd of onlookers to stand back and avoid trampling the garden.
b. The officer courteously asked the crowd of onlookers to stand back and to please avoid trampling the garden.

6.

a. To keep her daughter safe, the rat poison had to be locked away.
b. To keep her daughter safe, Sheryl had to lock the rat poison away.

7.

a. We prepared for our guest a special dish consisting of rice, sausage, and spicy peppers.
b. We prepared a special dish for our guest consisting of rice, sausage, and spicy peppers.

8.

a. For many asthma sufferers who also have allergies struggle during the spring.
b. Many asthma sufferers who also have allergies struggle during the spring.

9.

a. Every candidate must complete the exercises in the training manual before class tomorrow.
b. It is essential that every candidate must complete the exercises in the training manual before class tomorrow.

10.

a. To identify the correct punishment, listed in the appropriate section of the penal code.
b. The correct punishment is listed in the appropriate section of the penal code.

11.

a. Lawmakers hoped to decrease the rate of domestic violence by raising the penalty for first-time offenders.
b. Hoping to decrease the rate of domestic violence, the new law raised the penalty for first-time offenders.

12.

a. During the review of the investigation, the officers noticed some differences in the witness' stories were missed during the investigation.
b. During their review, the officers noticed that some differences in the witness' stories had been missed in the initial investigation.

13.

a. Darnell would learn that the benefits of restraint were much greater than those of impulsiveness.
b. Darnell would learn that the benefits of restraint were much greater than impulsiveness.

14.

a. The coroner, an essential position in the department, responsible for gathering forensic information from the deceased.
b. The coroner is an essential employee in the department, since he or she is responsible for gathering forensic information from the deceased.

15.

a. Francine felt that her daughter would not be protected until they moved to a new city.
b. Francine felt that her daughter's safety would not be protected until they moved to a new city.

16.

a. To find best practices for approaching erratic drivers, check the second chapter of the traffic stop manual.
b. To find best practices for approaching erratic drivers check the second chapter of the traffic stop manual.

17.

a. The police department has had a time finding new recruits in today's social climate.
b. The local police department has had a hard time finding new recruits in today's social climate.

18.

a. The officers ran the car's plates and notice they matched a stolen car.
b. The officers ran the car's plates and noticed they matched a stolen car.

Spelling

Instructions: In the following sentences, choose the correct spelling of the missing word.

19. Even though the last few weeks had been hard, Barry knew he had much to be ________ about in his life.

a. greatful
b. grateful
c. greatfull
d. gratefull

20. He always read the newspaper to see ________ there were any good jobs in the classified advertising section.

a. weather
b. wether
c. wather
d. whether

21. To be ________ in any endeavor, one must commit oneself entirely.

a. successful
b. succesful
c. successfull
d. sucesful

22. The manager hoped he could ________ last month's numbers without requiring any help from the rest of the department.

a. exeed
b. exceed
c. excede
d. exsede

23. Hiking, gardening, and bridge were more than enough to fill up all of her ________ time.

a. leesure
b. lesure
c. leisure
d. liesur

24. Even though he was an adult by any measure, Kevin nevertheless listened carefully to the ________ of his parents.

a. judgment
b. judgement
c. jugement
d. judgemente

25. A leader should never ________ the importance of earning the support of his or her followers.

a. undarrate
b. undarate
c. underate
d. underrate

26. The diner was understaffed, but the managers were still willing to _______ a large party of tourists.

a. acommodate
b. accommodate
c. acomodate
d. accomodate

27. The witness _______ that she had seen the suspect enter the residence through a bedroom window.

a. alledged
b. alleged
c. illeged
d. aledged

28. If the _______ is correct, we will have enough fuel to make it back to Sacramento.

a. gauge
b. gage
c. guage
d. gaug

29. The car should run for at least another hundred thousand miles, so long as you get all the usual _______.

a. maintenance
b. maintanance
c. meintenence
d. mentainance

30. After several hours of deliberation, the jury decided to _______ the defendant on all charges.

a. aquit
b. acuit
c. acquit
d. aqcuit

31. "Your performance on the exam should _______ you," the teacher sternly remarked to Sally.

a. embarrass
b. ambaress
c. embaress
d. embarass

32. Using your service _______ for personal business is typically forbidden by employers.

a. vehical
b. vehicle
c. vehickle
d. vihical

33. This award is given _______ to the officer who demonstrated the most bravery over the course of the last year.

a. anually
b. annally
c. annually
d. annully

34. Talking with _______ is a great way to learn new methods and strategies.

a. colleges
b. colleagues
c. collegues
d. coleagues

35. The public was captivated by the story of a mom who seemed to just _______ while on a run.

a. disapear
b. dissaper
c. disappear
d. dissappear

36. A ballistic _______ can be used to stop projectiles.

a. sheeld
b. shield
c. sheild
d. shild

Vocabulary

Instructions: In each of the following sentences, choose the word or phrase that most nearly has the same meaning as the underlined word.

37. He did not miss an opportunity to repudiate the charges that had been brought against him.

a. Confirm
b. Deny
c. Congratulate
d. Reform

38. Her inept handling of the case convinced her supervisors that she was not ready for a promotion.

a. Worthless
b. Valuable
c. Ferocious
d. Awkward

39. Dina received every possible plaudit from her bosses after her superlative conduct during the investigation.

a. Praise
b. Expertise
c. Focus
d. Contrast

40. After a five-year absence from the workplace, he discovered that some of his old methods were now obsolete.

a. Incorrect
b. Reckless
c. Special
d. Outdated

41. He must resolve to make the final ascent up the mountain, no matter how steep.

a. Delegate
b. Decide
c. Stagnate
d. Consider

42. She knew that her work problems were transient, but still she couldn't stop focusing on them to the point of distraction.

a. Impermanent
b. Fixed
c. Ghostly
d. Sedate

43. Florence knew she must <u>hasten</u> if she wanted to catch the final train of the day.

a. Delay
b. Accelerate
c. Flagellate
d. Forget

44. The recovery of millions of <u>counterfeit</u> dollars was a huge breakthrough in the case.

a. Coordinated
b. Supreme
c. Fake
d. Inferior

45. The room was already filled with bold and bright colors, so Sheila selected a more <u>neutral</u> tone for the walls.

a. Impartial
b. Life-Like
c. Belligerent
d. Social

46. Community service is sometimes <u>punitive</u>, but it can also be enriching and inspiring.

a. Disciplinary
b. Engaged
c. Trivial
d. Defamatory

47. He could barely concentrate on his work problems while his <u>domestic</u> life was in such disarray.

a. Nightly
b. Household
c. Buoyant
d. Tranquil

48. He begged the judge for a <u>reprieve</u>, but the evidence against him was too strong.

a. Mercy
b. Collect
c. Defend
d. Pay Back

49. The work in front of her was <u>tedious</u>, but she was determined to get through it all before lunch.

a. Exaggerated
b. Speedy
c. Cantankerous
d. Boring

50. The strongest perfume was not enough to nullify the aroma of the skunk.

a. Negate
b. Annoy
c. Defy
d. Accumulate

51. Being wealthy or famous does not preclude one from being the victim of fraud.

a. Extend
b. Prevent
c. Collect
d. Salivate

52. New officers often feel like they cannot voice their thoughts to superior officers.

a. Express
b. Control
c. Lend
d. Handle

53. The terrorist was stopped before he was able to plot a second attack.

a. Constitute
b. Devise
c. Share
d. Source

54. The shouts from protestors were incessant and made it hard to hear anything else.

a. Quiet
b. Fast
c. Dependable
d. Constant

Reading Comprehension

Refer to the following for questions 55–56:

Protective vests for law enforcement officers include ballistic-resistant and stab-resistant body armor that provides coverage and protection primarily for the torso. Different kinds of armor protect officers against different kinds of threats. Ballistic-resistant body armor protects against bullet penetrations and the blunt trauma associated with bullet impacts. These vests include soft body armor that protects against handgun bullets and less flexible tactical armor composed of soft and hard components that protect against rifle bullets. Stab-resistant body armor protects against knives and spikes. Manufacturers also make combination armor that protects against both types of threats. When purchasing body armor, law enforcement agencies must consider the kinds of threats their officers will likely face and choose body armor with suitable properties to protect against those threats.

55. Based on the preceding passage, which of the following statements is most accurate?

a. There are specialized types of body armor for different situations.
b. Stab-resistant body armor is useless against bullets.
c. Ballistic-resistant protective vests typically provide full-body coverage.
d. Law enforcement departments should all purchase the same type of protective vest.

56. Based on the preceding passage, which of the following statements is most accurate?

a. There are special forms of body armor for protecting the lower body.
b. Police officers must wear body armor at all times.
c. Body armor is effective in all situations.
d. The body armor that protects against handgun bullets is more flexible than the armor that protects against rifle bullets.

Refer to the following for questions 57–58:

Radio code is the coding system for identifying units both inside and outside the department. There are three components to every radio code. Each of these components must be included when officers are dispatched. In this coding system, units are identified with three characters: a number designating the severity, a letter designating the location, and a number identifying the type of event.

Severity	***Location***	***Event type***
1: Emergency	A: Northeast	1: Traffic offense
2: Urgent	B: North	2: Domestic dispute
3: Non-urgent	C: Northwest	3: Public disorder
	D: West	4: Drug offense
	E: Southwest	
	F: South	
	G: Southeast	
	H: East	

57. Using the above coding system, the call number 3-C-4 would signify:

a. A non-urgent drug offense in the northwestern part of the city
b. An emergency traffic offense in the western part of the city
c. A non-urgent domestic dispute in the southeastern part of the city
d. An urgent public disorder in the southern part of the city

58. Using the above coding system, the call number 1-G-2 would signify:

a. An urgent traffic offense in the southeastern part of the city
b. An emergency traffic offense in the eastern part of the city
c. A domestic dispute emergency in the southeastern part of the city
d. A non-urgent drug offense in the northern part of the city

Refer to the following for questions 59–60:

Because concern for elder abuse as a criminal issue is a fairly recent development, there are gaps in our knowledge about the extent and causes of such abuse. The majority of research on elder mistreatment has focused on victims; the motivations of abusers and the relationship between abusers and victims have received little attention. This produces an incomplete picture of the dynamics fueling elder abuse. Also, the field of research has relied heavily on the caregiver stress model, which holds that elder abuse can be attributed to the stress associated with providing care and assistance to frail, highly dependent elderly people. However, this model does not fit all situations and types of elder abuse. The field lacks an adequate guiding theory to explain the range of causes behind elder abuse and promote systematic data collection.

59. Based on the preceding passage, which of the following statements is most accurate?

a. Research based on the caregiver stress model has generated sufficient amounts of data.
b. There is still a great deal of research to be done on elder abuse.
c. Most research on elder abuse has focused on the motivations of abusers.
d. The caregiver stress model fails to address the cause of elder abuse.

60. Based on the preceding passage, which of the following statements is most accurate?

a. Not all elder abuse is caused by the stress of caring for the elderly.
b. The caregiver stress model is the most recent explanation for elder abuse.
c. Most research on elder abuse has focused on the relationship between abusers and victims.
d. The caregiver stress model is never appropriate for describing elder abuse.

Refer to the following for questions 61–62:

When a loved one is sentenced to prison, the emotional turmoil is difficult for everyone to handle. Perhaps the heaviest burden is felt by those who are unintentional victims of crime—children of incarcerated parents. Nationally, 7.3 million children have at least one parent in jail or prison. Sadly, 70% of these kids are doomed to follow in the same footsteps as their parents by becoming imprisoned at some point in their lives. In fact, children of incarcerated parents are five times more likely than their peers to commit crimes. However, these at-risk children are largely ignored before they get in trouble.

61. Based on the preceding passage, which of the following statements is most accurate?

a. The children of incarcerated parents are no more likely than other children to be imprisoned later in life.
b. The children of incarcerated parents should not receive special treatment.
c. Children with both parents in jail are even more likely than children with one parent in jail to be imprisoned later in life.
d. More than half of the children of incarcerated parents will be imprisoned at some point during their lives.

62. Based on the preceding passage, which of the following statements is most accurate?

a. The spouses of incarcerated people are not defined as unintentional victims of crime.
b. The children of incarcerated parents receive no special treatment at present.
c. The children of incarcerated parents are more likely than other children to commit crimes at some point in their lives.
d. More than 7 million children of incarcerated parents will themselves end up in jail.

Refer to the following for question 63:

Specialized responses to people with mental illnesses are an outgrowth of community policing, and as such, should reflect a partnership between a law enforcement agency and other stakeholder groups and individuals. Partners for the lead law enforcement agency should include mental health service providers, people with mental illnesses and their family members and loved ones, and mental health advocates. Any stakeholder may initiate the planning for the specialized response, but to take root, the lead law enforcement agency must fully embrace the effort.

63. Based on the preceding passage, which of the following statements is most accurate?

a. Most law enforcement agencies are able by themselves to create effective policies for responding to the mentally ill.
b. Planning a department's response to the mentally ill requires cooperation from several parties.
c. Only the law enforcement agency can initiate the planning for a specialized response.
d. The law enforcement agency is the most important party in planning the specialized response to the mentally ill.

Refer to the following for questions 64–65:

Routine activity theory suggests that crime occurs when a motivated offender, a suitable target, and the lack of a capable guardian converge in the same place at the same time. Criminals choose or find their targets within the context of their routine activities, such as traveling to and from work, or other activities such as shopping, and tend not to go too far out of their way to commit crimes.

64. Based on the preceding passage, which of the following statements is most accurate?

a. The routine activity theory suggests that criminals operate in or near the places they already frequent.
b. The work of a ring of sophisticated jewel thieves could be explained by the routine activity theory of crime.
c. Routine activity theory suggests that most crime is committed by relatives of the victim.
d. The routine activity theory does not account for the problem of employee theft.

65. According to the information in the passage, which of the following crimes could be explained by routine activity theory?

a. A woman accidentally hits a pedestrian on her drive to work.
b. A presidential candidate is assassinated at a rally.
c. A man is robbed while taking his afternoon walk.
d. An art thief steals a famous painting from the Louvre.

Refer to the following for questions 66–67:

Federal law prohibits the sale of firearms or ammunition to juveniles and people who have been convicted of felonies and some violent misdemeanors. Federally mandated background checks keep these people from buying firearms at licensed dealers. Prohibited buyers may turn to the largely unregulated secondary market: gun sales between private individuals. The secondary market is a major source of guns used in crimes.

Why do people buy guns illegally? While some may buy them with the intent of using them in a crime, reasons can vary. Boston's Operation Ceasefire, a successful gun violence intervention, found that youths frequently acquire guns because they're afraid of being a target of violence from others.

66. Based on the preceding passage, which of the following statements is most accurate?

a. Juveniles are allowed to purchase ammunition in some states.
b. The federal government should eliminate background checks to reduce the illegal sale of firearms.
c. The federal government regulates the secondary gun market.
d. Background checks prevent juveniles and convicted criminals from purchasing guns at licensed stores.

67. Based on the preceding passage, which of the following statements is most accurate?

a. People illegally purchase guns for many reasons.
b. Guns purchased from licensed dealers are a part of the secondary market.
c. Gun sales between private individuals are mostly used for criminal activity.
d. Most of the people who purchase guns illegally do so for protection.

Refer to the following for questions 68–69:

You could call this scam a license to steal, and it certainly was, until it all came crashing down on the corrupt state employees and their accomplices who were selling California driver's licenses for cash. For at least three years, though, between 2009 and 2012, the scammers had a nearly seamless operation that netted a tidy profit. Here's how it worked: A man who owned a driving school let his students know that—for a price—he could guarantee them a license, even if they had already failed the driving test. Often, they didn't even have to take the test, thanks to the man's connections at the Department of Motor Vehicles (DMV) office in El Cajon, California. Those willing to pay anywhere from $500 to $2,500 to corrupt DMV employees could get a license with no questions asked.

68. Based on the preceding passage, which of the following statements is most accurate?

a. Students received fake exam results for free.
b. The owner of a California driving school and DMV employees conspired to falsify the results of exams.
c. The scam began in 2008.
d. This scam would only have been possible in California.

69. Based on the preceding passage, which of the following statements is most accurate?

a. Driving schools should be administered by the state.
b. The state of California issues licenses to steal.
c. This scam made driving more dangerous in California.
d. A California driver's license usually costs at least $500.

Refer to the following for questions 70–71:

Public efforts to restrict firepower among those most prone to violence generally focus only on guns, not ammunition. For example, firearms dealers run the names of would-be gun buyers through an instant background check system to verify whether the person is legally allowed to own a gun. But although the same restrictions technically apply, ammunition purchasers are not subject to the same background check. This means that people who shouldn't be able to buy ammunition might be doing just that.

Research on illegal gun markets in the streets of Chicago shows that criminals already have a more difficult time buying ammunition than buying guns. If retail sales of ammunition were more tightly controlled to keep ammunition from falling into the wrong hands, would this squeeze the illegal market even further, and, perhaps, reduce gun violence?

70. Based on the preceding passage, which of the following statements is most accurate?

a. People who are not allowed to buy firearms may be allowed to purchase ammunition.
b. The legal efforts to reduce gun violence have focused primarily on ammunition.
c. A background check is required for the purchase of ammunition.
d. Ammunition is easier to purchase than guns themselves.

71. Based on the preceding passage, which of the following statements is most accurate?

a. One way to reduce gun violence may be to control ammunition sales more tightly.
b. There has been a sharp decline in gun violence in Chicago.
c. It can be difficult to find the right ammunition for automatic weapons.
d. Gun violence is the most common crime in Chicago.

Refer to the following for questions 72–73:

There is good evidence that early interventions in childhood, such as home visits by nurses, preschool intellectual enrichment programs, and parent management training, are effective in preventing delinquency. For example, an evaluation of the Elmira (NY) Nurse-Family Partnership program found that at age 15, children of the higher-risk mothers who received home visits had significantly fewer arrests than control populations. Another follow-up when the children were 19 showed that the daughters (but not the sons) of mothers who received home visits had significantly fewer arrests and convictions.

72. Based on the preceding passage, which of the following statements is most accurate?

a. Juvenile delinquency is the fault of parents.
b. Delinquency cannot be totally eradicated.
c. Juvenile delinquency mostly affects urban communities.
d. Efforts to prevent juvenile delinquency should begin when children are very young.

73. Based on the preceding passage, which of the following statements is most accurate?

a. Boys are more likely to be juvenile delinquents than girls.
b. Parent management training should be mandatory.
c. Elmira has the highest rate of juvenile delinquency in New York.
d. The sons of mothers who had home visits did not have significantly fewer arrests and convictions at age 19.

Refer to the following for questions 74–75:

Training must be provided to improve officers' responses to people with mental illnesses. Agencies may differ in the amount of training they offer: some will provide comprehensive training to all officers, some will provide this training only to a subset, and some will provide basic training to everyone in combination with more comprehensive training to a subset. At a minimum, a group of officers sufficient to cover all time shifts and geographic districts should receive extensive skills and knowledge training that builds on the more cursory information routinely given on this topic at recruit and in-service trainings. The chief law enforcement executive should ensure that training is also provided to supervisory and support personnel, such as midlevel managers, field training officers, call takers, and dispatchers, who advance the specialized program's operations.

74. Based on the preceding passage, which of the following statements is most accurate?

a. Training for dealing with the mentally ill may be restricted to the officers who serve a particular geographic district.
b. There is a standard training protocol for dealing with the mentally ill.
c. Officers need special training to serve the mentally ill.
d. In-service training never includes advice for dealing with the mentally ill.

75. Based on the preceding passage, what conclusion can be safely drawn?

a. All officers should receive extensive training on how to respond to people with mental illnesses.
b. Mentally ill people pose more of a threat than people without mental illness.
c. Support personnel do not need training on mental illness.
d. An officer with extensive training on how to respond to people with mental illness should be available at all times.

Refer to the following for question 76:

A police force with integrity is one with little or no misconduct or corruption. In the past, most studies viewed the problem of misconduct as one of individual problem officers, the so-called bad apples on the force. More recent studies show that white people generally see misconduct as episodic and confined to individual officers, while black people tend to see misconduct as a more entrenched aspect of policing.

76. Based on the preceding passage, which of the following statements is most accurate?

a. A police force may have strong integrity and yet be filled with corruption.
b. A white person would be more apt to see officer misconduct as inherent to the law enforcement system.
c. Black people are more likely to be the victims of officer misconduct.
d. White people and black people tend to view police misconduct differently.

Refer to the following for questions 77–78:

Child abductions require quick reaction by law enforcement officers, but there are occasions in which the general public becomes involved. AMBER Alerts are issued to citizens in the area surrounding an abduction so that they may assist in locating the victim and perpetrator; however, an AMBER Alert can only be issued if the abduction meets all of the following criteria.

First, there must be reasonable belief by officers that an abduction has actually occurred. The possibility that the child has run away or left willingly must be eliminated. This is usually done through speaking with eyewitnesses and family members. It must also be believed that the child is in danger of death or serious injury. There must be sufficient descriptive information about both the victim and the abductor to provide information crucial to recovery. This can include physical descriptions of both parties and information about the vehicle used in the abduction. The victim of the kidnapping must be 17 years of age or younger in order for an AMBER Alert to be issued. The name of the child and related critical information must be entered into the National Crime Information Center.

If an abduction fulfills all of these requirements, an AMBER Alert can be issued across radio and TV broadcasts as well as to cellphones in the area. The alerts may also appear on road signs and other digital signage. As the list of criteria is long, and time is of the essence with solving these kinds of cases, officers must think quickly and use their best judgment to determine if an abduction qualifies for an AMBER Alert.

77. Based on the preceding passage, which of the following statements is most accurate?

a. AMBER Alerts broadcast the disappearance of all youths.
b. AMBER Alerts are primarily intended to inform officers not yet involved in a case.
c. AMBER Alerts are sent to network subscribers only.
d. AMBER Alerts have stringent requirements for issuance.

78. Based on the preceding passage, which of the following statements is most accurate?

a. Whether or not an abduction meets some of the listed criteria is up to the discretion of the responding officers.
b. Officers must collect information and write a detailed report to use in determining if the abduction qualifies for an AMBER Alert.
c. Because of the established criteria, it is not necessary for officers to use their own judgment when responding to an abduction.
d. The victim's family is able to report abductions directly to the AMBER Network and have an alert issued.

Refer to the following for questions 79–80:

It is estimated that there are over 25 million human trafficking victims worldwide. Being able to identify these victims is the first step in freeing them. While sex trafficking is often the first thought that springs to mind when discussing trafficking, labor trafficking can be just as dangerous, and these victims are often in plain sight. Victims can be found in any setting where workers are needed, such as in construction, agriculture, cleaning services, retail, and food service. Law enforcement officers should be aware of the red flags that may indicate that someone is a victim of labor trafficking. Individuals living with their employer or with several other employees in a small space is a general indicator of trafficking. When asked about living conditions or arrangements, victims may be hesitant to answer, or their answers may sound rehearsed. Many victims do not have access to their identification, passport, or other government documents. These are typically kept by their trafficker to exercise control and to prevent victims from being able to leave. Being unaware of where they are geographically and being transported to and from work by an employer may also indicate trafficking. Having an overall fearful and guarded response when discussing their job is also cause for suspicion. Cases of labor trafficking should be investigated carefully so that the physical safety of victims is maintained and so that traffickers can be held responsible.

79. Based on the preceding passage, which of the following statements is most accurate?

a. Labor trafficking victims are less common than sex trafficking victims.
b. Labor trafficking victims are likely to be forthcoming with information regarding their employer.
c. Labor trafficking victims are often seen in manual labor and service positions.
d. Labor trafficking usually occurs behind closed doors, such as in factories.

80. Based on the preceding passage, which of the following statements is most accurate?

a. A trafficking victim will likely not be able to provide any documentation regarding their identity.
b. Victims of trafficking are usually free outside of work hours.
c. Traffickers do not provide transportation to the work environment.
d. An individual being trafficked may choose to leave the environment.

Refer to the following for questions 81–82:

Community policing is a strategy used to develop relationships between officers and community members in areas with high crime rates. It is intended to prevent crimes from happening as opposed to reacting when they do. Having the same officers present in a particular area allows them to become familiar with individuals in the community, leading to the relationships needed for their involvement. Involving the community in problem solving is a large component of community policing. This allows community members to provide their own perspectives on the activities and issues occurring around them. The information they provide is used to collaboratively develop solutions to these problems. Research has shown that community policing is more effective in decreasing crime than the more traditional, reactive approaches. It increases the public's trust in law enforcement and decreases overall crime rates.

81. Based on the preceding passage, which of the following statements is most accurate?

a. Traditional approaches to policing are as effective as community policing.
b. Community policing tends to damage trust between members in the community.
c. Being proactive is a key component to community policing.
d. Officers that participate in community policing are selected by community members.

82. Based on the preceding passage, which of the following statements is most accurate?

a. Increased patrol in particular communities is linked to a decrease in crime.
b. Relationships are a pillar in community policing.
c. Officers that participate in community policing are held to different standards.
d. Community members are expected to adhere to strategies developed by officers.

Cloze

(83) ____ began as a routine traffic stop turned into a thirty-minute, high-speed chase for Officer Terry Johnson. Officer Johnson was patrolling (84) ___ stretch of highway just east of Waterboro when he observed a car traveling slightly faster than the (85) _____ limit, which in that area was fifty-five miles per (86) ____. As the car passed by, Officer (87) _______ noticed that the car had a broken left taillight.

Officer Johnson turned (88) __ his siren and pulled onto the highway behind the vehicle. At (89) _____, it appeared that the driver would comply. The car pulled off the (90) ____ onto the gravel shoulder and came to a (91) ____. Officer Johnson noted the license plate number, gathered his equipment, (92) ___ exited his service vehicle. Once he was approximately ten feet (93) ____ from the car, however, the driver suddenly restarted his vehicle and drove away (94) __ great speed. Officer Johnson attempted to shoot out the back tire of the vehicle, (95) ___ his shots bounced off the gravel to either side.

Flustered, Officer Johnson ran back to his service vehicle and immediately called for back-up. Then, he shifted the (96) ___ into drive and sped off in pursuit. The fleeing vehicle (97) ___ about a quarter mile ahead of him when he began, but he quickly made (98) __ the distance with his siren blaring and lights flashing. The suspect vehicle, however, did not stop (99) ____ he drew near behind it. Instead, it took a quick turn (100) ___ the highway and on to a side street.

At this point, Officer Johnson had a decision (101) __ make. (102)______ he continue with his pursuit and risk endangering other drivers and pedestrians by driving at high speed through a congested area, or should he rely on his back-up and the surveillance abilities (103) __ the department? He decided to continue with his pursuit, at (104) _____ until his colleagues could get organized and join the chase. Already, he (105) _____ hear on the radio that a helicopter had taken off at department headquarters and was approaching the neighborhood of the chase. Officer Johnson knew (106) ____ the chopper would be able to find the suspect more quickly if he stayed close because the pilot could use the signal from the patrol car (107) ___ guidance.

As all this was going on, the suspect and Officer Johnson continued to weave (108) _______ traffic. There were a couple of close (109) _____. At one point, the suspect drove up on the sidewalk slightly, and a couple of middle-aged pedestrians had to jump up onto the stoop of a house in order to avoid (110) _____ hit. Officer Johnson focused (111) ___ concentration on maintaining visual contact with the car, and with driving as safely (112) __ possible. He hoped (113) ____ his fellow officers would be able to end the chase, which had already gone on for more than twenty (114) _______.

Finally, (115) __ he rounded a narrow turn, Officer Johnson saw a roadblock ahead. (116) ___ heart leapt with joy. (117) __ avoid a fatal accident, the suspect had no choice but to (118) ____. Guns drawn, several officers raced to apprehend the driver, who exited the car with his (119) _____ raised, resigned to his fate. An inspection of the (120) ___ revealed several automatic weapons and a duffel bag full of illegal narcotics. Officer Johnson later received a commendation (121) ____ the department for his performance (122) ______ the chase.

Reasoning

Instructions: Officers often face situations in which they need to determine how different pieces of information relate to one another. In this section, you will be presented with information such as a group or ordered series of facts, numbers, letters, or words. Your task is to study the various pieces of information and try to understand how they relate to one another.

123. Three of the following words are similar, while one is different. Select the one that is different.

a. Glad
b. Well
c. Happily
d. Quickly

124. Identify the next number in the sequence: 3, 5, 8, 10, 13, 15...

a. 17
b. 18
c. 19
d. 20

125. Denise is three months older than Ellen, who is two months younger than Francesca. Gertrude is four months older than Francesca. Who is the oldest?

a. Denise
b. Francesca
c. Gertrude
d. Ellen

126. Identify the next number in the sequence: 4, 6, 8, 4, 6, 8...

a. 4
b. 6
c. 8
d. 10

127. Sally, Fred, and Mary are siblings. Fred is ten years older than Mary, and Sally is twice as old as Mary. How old is Mary?

a. 12
b. 16
c. 22
d. Not enough information

128. Three of the following words are similar, while one is different. Select the one that is different.

a. Colombia
b. Connecticut
c. Delaware
d. Wyoming

129. Identify the next number in the sequence: 772, 727, 277, 772...

a. 277
b. 727
c. 772
d. Not enough information

130. Doris, Erma, and Francine are in a pie-eating contest. Doris eats seven pies, and Francine eats four fewer. Erma eats three more pies than Francine. How many pies does Erma eat?

a. 4
b. 5
c. 6
d. Not enough information

131. On their last French test, Jamal got a higher score than Lindsay, and Lindsay got a higher score than Soo Yin. Jamal's score was slightly higher than Bert's. Who got the second-highest score in the class?

a. Lindsay
b. Bert
c. Soo Yin
d. Not enough information

Answer Key and Explanations for Test #2

Clarity

1. B: The other version of the sentence has a confusing mixture of verb tenses. In particular, the auxiliary verb *must* is awkward, because it suggests that Frank remembered that he had to go back *and* remembered that he had to retrieve the credit card simultaneously. In the correct version of the sentence, the word *so* demonstrates that having to go back to the store was a consequence of remembering that the card had been left behind.

2. A: The other version omits the commas, which indicate how the sentence is to be read. Even without the commas, the sentence is comprehensible, but appropriate punctuation encourages the reader to make the appropriate pauses. By signaling the rhythm of the sentence, punctuation improves clarity.

3. B: The other version of the sentence does not maintain a consistent structure as it lists the things he did in pursuit of the suspect. The addition of the preposition *through* complicates the reader's progress through the sentence. In addition, "dodging" red lights does not totally make sense. In the clearer version, an appropriate verb has been paired with each obstacle, and the sentence is much smoother.

4. A: The other version is too wordy. Specifically, the phrase "The reason... was because" is unnecessary. In the correct version of the sentence, this awkward construction has been removed and the result is a much smoother sentence.

5. A: The other version is incorrect because it misuses the word *please*. The sentence is used to describe what the officer is doing generally, not what the officer is saying specifically. By inserting the word *please* into the final phrase, the sentence seems like it is acting more like a quotation instead of a description, confusing the meaning of the sentence.

6. B: In the other version, the awkward use of the introductory clause makes it sound as if the rat poison was trying to keep her daughter safe. Of course, this would not be the interpretation of most readers, but nevertheless the sentence fails to identify the subject of the introductory clause. In the correct version, the subject is clear.

7. A: In the incorrect version, it sounds as if the guest rather than the dish consisted of rice, sausage, and spicy peppers. By rearranging the clauses, the correct version makes the meaning clear.

8. B: In the other version, the word *for* at the beginning is unnecessary. In fact, the addition of this word turns the sentence into a fragment.

9. A: The other version of the sentence is too wordy. Specifically, the phrase *it is essential* and the word *must* are redundant. The correct version of the sentence eliminates "it is essential that," and there is no change to the sentence's meaning. The sentence could also be written, "It is essential that every candidate complete the exercises...," but this version is slightly less concise than the correct version in this question.

10. B: The other version is a fragment because it does not have a subject. A reader would probably be able to make sense of the incorrect version, but the absence of proper grammar would be distracting.

11. A: The other version is incorrect because it sounds as if the new law was hoping, when of course a law cannot hope.

12. B: The other repeats the word investigation, which is redundant and clumsy. This sort of repetition slows the reader down and may lead to confusion. The correct version avoids this problem.

13. A: In the other version of the sentence, the terms of the comparison are unclear. It appears to be saying that the benefits of restraint are better than impulsiveness itself, rather than the *benefits* of impulsiveness. This makes some sense, but it seems more likely that the author is trying to compare the benefits of restraint with the benefits of impulsiveness. The correct version of the sentence makes this comparison more apparent.

14. B: The other version has a couple of problems. To begin with, it is a fragment because it does not have a main verb. To be grammatically correct, the sentence would have to state, "The coroner...*is* responsible." Another problem with this sentence is that the subordinate clause refers to the coroner as a position rather than as a person. There are cases where it would be appropriate to discuss the coroner as a position rather than a person, but in this case the focus is on the tasks performed by the coroner, and tasks are performed by a person, not a job role.

15. A: The other version refers to protecting her daughter's safety, which makes less sense than simply protecting her daughter.

16. A: A comma is needed to separate the dependent clause "to find the best practices for approaching erratic drivers" from the independent clause "check the second chapter of the traffic stop manual." Omitting a comma turns the statement into a run-on sentence.

17. B: The other version lacks adjectives, which provide necessary clarity. The use of *local* and *hard* tells the reader where the department is and better explains their experience in finding new recruits.

18. B: The sentence uses the past tense verb *ran*, so other verbs in the sentence should also be past tense. *Notice* is present tense, while *noticed* is past tense.

Spelling

19. B: grateful

20. D: whether

21. A: successful

22. B: exceed

23. C: leisure

24. A: judgment

25. D: underrate

26. B: accommodate

27. B: alleged

28. A: gauge

29. A: maintenance

30. C: acquit

31. A: embarrass

32. B: vehicle

33. C: annually

34. B: colleagues

35. C: disappear

36. B: shield

Vocabulary

37. B: *Deny* most nearly has the same meaning as *repudiate*. Both of these verbs mean to reject or turn one's back on.

38. D: *Awkward* most nearly has the same meaning as *inept*. Both of these adjectives mean something like clumsy, improper, or lacking in skill.

39. A: *Praise* most nearly has the same meaning as *plaudit*. Both of them refer to positive feedback or comments.

40. D: *Outdated* most nearly has the same meaning as *obsolete*. These adjectives both mean that something is old-fashioned and, specifically, not able to be used anymore because of its age, and because subsequent advances have made it useless.

41. B: *Decide* most nearly has the same meaning as *resolve*. Both of these verbs mean to make a choice.

42. A: *Impermanent* most nearly has the same meaning as *transient*. Both of these words refer to things that are passing or that will not exist for very long.

43. B: *Accelerate* most nearly has the same meaning as *hasten*. Both of them mean to speed up or increase the rate.

44. C: *Fake* most nearly has the same meaning as *counterfeit*. Both of these words are used to describe things that have been falsified or forged.

45. A: *Impartial* most nearly has the same meaning as *neutral*. Both of them mean not taking a side.

46. A: *Disciplinary* most nearly has the same meaning as *punitive*. Both of these words indicate the negative consequences of misdeeds.

47. B: *Household* most nearly has the same meaning as *domestic*. Both of these words refer to things that are done in one's own area, as opposed to in a foreign or non-native area.

48. A: *Mercy* most nearly has the same meaning as *reprieve*. Both of them mean a release from punishment or trouble.

49. D: *Boring* most nearly has the same meaning as *tedious*. Both of them mean uninteresting.

50. A: *Negate* most nearly has the same meaning as *nullify*. Both of these words mean to erase or reduce to nothing.

51. B: *Prevent* most nearly has the same meaning as *preclude*. Both of these words mean to act ahead of time to keep something from happening.

52. A: *Express* has the closest meaning to *voice.* Both words mean "to speak out."

53. B: *Devise* has the closest meaning to *plot.* Both words mean "to plan something."

54. D: *Constant* has the closest meaning to *incessant.* Both words mean "to continue without pause."

Reading Comprehension

55. A: Based on the passage, the most accurate statement is that there are specialized types of body armor for different situations. The passage makes this plain in the second sentence: "Different kinds of armor protect officers against different kinds of threats." The specialization of protective vests does not necessarily mean that these vests will provide no protection against other attacks; for instance, the passage does not state that stab-resistant body armor will be useless against bullets, merely that there are more specialized types of armor for this purpose. The first sentence indicates that protective vests generally cover the torso, and not the entire body. Finally, the main idea of the passage is that law enforcement departments should not all purchase the same protective vests, but should select the appropriate vests based on the hazards their officers are likely to encounter.

56. D: Based on the passage, the most accurate statement is that the body armor that protects against handgun bullets is more flexible than the armor that protects against rifle bullets. The passage indicates as much when it states that the tactical armor designed to protect against rifle bullets is "less flexible." There probably are special forms of body armor for protecting the lower body, but the passage does not mention them. It also does not state that police officers must wear body armor at all times. Finally, the passage does not suggest that body armor is effective in all situations.

57. A: Using the above coding system, the call number 3-C-4 would signify a non-urgent drug offense in the northwestern part of the city.

58. C: Using the above coding system, the call number 1-G-2 would signify a domestic dispute emergency in the southeastern part of the city.

59. B: Based on the passage, the most accurate statement is that there is still a great deal of research to be done on elder abuse. This is the main point of the passage, and is expressed in the first sentence: "there are gaps in our knowledge about the extent and causes of such abuse." The passage states that the caregiver stress model has not produced enough data, though it does address one of the causes of elder abuse (namely, the stress associated with caring for the elderly). Finally, the second sentence of the passage states that most research thus far has focused on the victims rather than the motivations of abusers.

60. A: Based on the passage, the most accurate statement is that not all elder abuse is caused by the stress of caring for the elderly. The caregiver stress model focuses on this cause, but the passage is clear that this explanation is inadequate for every situation. The passage does not state that the caregiver stress model is the most recent explanation for elder abuse, just that it is currently the most popular. The passage states that "little attention" has been paid to the relationship between abusers and victims. Finally, while the passage is clear that the caregiver stress model is not enough to explain every aspect of elder abuse, there is no suggestion that it is never appropriate for describing elder abuse.

61. D: Based on the passage, the most accurate statement is that more than half of the children of incarcerated parents will be imprisoned at some point during their lives. The passage states that 70% of these children will be imprisoned at some point. It also states that these children are five times more likely than their peers to commit crimes, which suggests that they are also more likely to go to jail. The passage does not state explicitly that children of incarcerated parents should receive special treatment, though the facts presented certainly lead to this conclusion. Finally, there is no mention that children with both parents in jail are even more likely than children with one parent in jail to be imprisoned later in life.

62. C: Based on the passage, the most accurate statement is that the children of incarcerated parents are more likely than other children to commit crimes at some point in their lives. According to the passage, in fact, the children of incarcerated parents are five times more likely than their peers to commit crimes. The spouses of incarcerated people could probably be defined as the unintentional victims of crime, but this passage does not do so. Rather, it identifies the children of the incarcerated as such. The passage does not state that these at-risk children receive no special treatment, though it does say that they are "largely ignored." Finally, the passage does not state that more than 7 million children of incarcerated parents will be imprisoned at some point. The passage does state that there are 7.3 million children with at least one parent in jail, but of these, only 70% (a little over 5 million) will end up in jail themselves.

63. B: Based on the passage, the most accurate statement is that planning a department's response to the mentally ill requires cooperation from several parties. The passage states that the specialized response protocol "should reflect a partnership between a law enforcement agency and other stakeholder groups and individuals." The passage is clear that law enforcement departments are not able to create these policies on their own, but that they are a collaboration with several parties. Moreover, the passage does not state that this planning must be initiated by the law enforcement department itself. Finally, there is no indication that the law enforcement agency is the most important party in planning the specialized response; on the contrary, the passage is clear that there are many stakeholders.

64. A: Based on the passage, the most accurate statement is that the routine activity theory suggests that criminals operate in or near the places they already frequent. This is evident in the second sentence: "Criminals choose or find their targets within the context of their routine activities." The routine activity theory probably would not be a very good explanation of the work of a ring of sophisticated jewel thieves, since these groups would necessarily be working in many different places, and not just those with which they were normally acquainted. The routine activity theory would, however, account for the problem of employee theft, since this is a crime committed by people who are very familiar with the work setting. This passage does not state that routine activity theory suggests that most crime is committed by relatives of the victim.

65. C: According to the passage, routine activity theory centers around the idea that crime occurs during routine activities when three elements converge: a motivated offender, a suitable target, and the lack of capable guardian coverage. In option C, the man is robbed during his daily routine in a location with little security. Although option A also occurs during a routine activity, the offender is not motivated to hit the pedestrian, as indicated by the word "accidentally." Options B and D are incorrect because, although they have motivated offenders and suitable targets, both involve high security and do not occur during routine events.

66. D: Based on the passage, the most accurate statement is that background checks prevent juveniles and convicted criminals from purchasing guns at licensed stores. Of course, these people often acquire guns from other sources. The passage states that juveniles are prevented from purchasing ammunition by federal law, which would apply in every state. There is no suggestion that background checks should be eliminated. While this would perhaps reduce illegal sales, it would only be because juveniles and felons would be able to obtain guns through the normal channels. Finally, the passage states explicitly that the secondary gun market is largely unregulated.

67. A: Based on the passage, the most accurate statement is that people illegally purchase guns for many reasons. This is expressed in the second sentence of the second paragraph. The guns purchased from licensed dealers are part of the primary market. The passage does not suggest that gun sales between private individuals are mostly used for criminal activity. Finally, the passage mentions that some illegal gun purchases are made for protection, but does not argue that this is the reason for most of these purchases.

68. B: Based on the passage, the most accurate statement is that the owner of a California driving school and DMV employees conspired to falsify the results of exams. This passage describes a scheme that required the participation of both the driving school operator and state employees. The article indicates that applicants paid at least $500 for a license, and that the scam began in 2009. There is no suggestion that this scam would only have been possible in California.

69. C: Based on the passage, the most accurate statement is that this scam made driving more dangerous in the state of California. The article states that the scam enabled drivers to obtain a license "even if they had already failed the driving test." There is no suggestion in the passage that driving schools should be administered by the state. The state of California does not literally issue licenses to steal. Finally, the California driver's license does not cost $500; this was the lower end of the range charged by the scammers for unearned licenses.

70. D: Based on the passage, the most accurate statement is that ammunition is easier to purchase than guns themselves. The first paragraph describes how would-be buyers of ammunition are not subjected to the same background check as if they were purchasing a gun. These people are actually forbidden from buying ammunition as well as firearms, but the current laws are ineffective at preventing ammunition sales. The first sentence of the passage states that public efforts thus far have focused primarily on guns, not ammunition.

71. A: Based on the passage, the most accurate statement is that one way to reduce gun violence may be to control ammunition sales more tightly. This suggestion is made in the final sentence of the passage. There is no indication in the passage that there has been a sharp decline in gun violence in Chicago, or that gun violence is the most common crime there. Neither is there any suggestion that it can be difficult to find the right ammunition for automatic weapons.

72. D: Based on the passage, the most accurate statement is that efforts to prevent juvenile delinquency should begin when children are very young. The first sentence indicates that these early interventions can be crucial in reducing later misbehavior. There is no suggestion that delinquency is the fault of parents, although the passage is clear that parents have a major role in preventing delinquency. Similarly, it seems unlikely that juvenile delinquency could be totally eradicated, but the passage does not address this question. Finally, the passage does not state that juvenile delinquency mostly affects urban communities.

73. D: Based on the passage, the most accurate statement is that the sons of mothers who had home visits did not have significantly fewer arrests and convictions at age 19. However, the passage does indicate that the daughters of these mothers did have fewer arrests and convictions. Still, the description of this research does not suggest that boys are more likely to be juvenile delinquents than girls. The passage does not argue that parent management training should be mandatory, though this might be inferred from the results of the research. Finally, the passage does not suggest that Elmira has the highest rate of juvenile delinquency in New York; it was simply the site of the research.

74. C: Based on the passage, the most accurate statement is that officers need special training to serve the mentally ill. The first sentence makes this statement, and the rest of the passage supports it. The passage does not state that training may be restricted to the officers who serve a particular geographic district; rather, it suggests that there should be trained officers for all times and places within the jurisdiction. The passage also suggests that there are different types and levels of training for officers in different positions. Finally, the passage directly states that basic information about dealing with the mentally ill is provided during recruit and in-service trainings.

75. D: The passage directly states that there should be enough officers with extensive training on this matter to cover all shifts and geographic areas. This would mean that an officer with appropriate training would be available at all times. In addition, the passage states that this is the minimum number of officers who should receive extensive training, meaning not all officers must receive such in-depth training, as option A suggests. Option B is incorrect because the passage never states why special training is needed for responding to people with mental illness, nor does it state that they pose more or less of a threat than others.

76. D: Based on the passage, the most accurate statement is that White people and Black people tend to view police misconduct differently. The last sentence of the passage indicates that White people view officer misconduct as a problem with individual officers, while Black people view it as a natural part of an unjust system. Based on the first sentence, it seems that a police force could not have integrity and be corrupt at the same time. Black people, not white people, are more apt to see officer misconduct as inherent to the law enforcement system. Finally, the passage does not indicate whether Black or White people are more likely to be the victims of officer misconduct.

77. D: Based on the passage, the most accurate statement is that AMBER Alerts have stringent requirements for issuance. If a case fails to fulfill any of the outlined criteria, it does not qualify for an AMBER Alert. Choice A is incorrect because alerts are not issued for youths when it cannot be concluded that they were abducted, or when they are not in danger. AMBER Alerts are meant to inform the public in the area of the abduction to be on the lookout for the victim and offender. Unlike what is stated in choice B, they are not meant for officers. These alerts are broadcasted on TV, radio, and digitally enabled devices. The passage does not suggest they require a network subscription or opt-in as choice C suggests.

78. A: Based on the passage, the most accurate statement is that whether or not an abduction meets some of the listed criteria is up to the discretion of the responding officers. Officers are responsible for determining if an abduction truly did occur and if the child is in danger. They must use their own judgment, contrary to what is stated in choice C. Choice B is incorrect because a written report is not used when determining if an abduction qualifies for an AMBER Alert. The passage does not suggest that families are able to initiate these reports on their own like choice D suggests.

79. C: Based on the passage, the most accurate statement is that labor trafficking victims are often seen in manual labor and service positions. The passage cites the fields of construction, agriculture, cleaning services, retail, and food service as examples of common places where labor trafficking occurs. Choice A cannot be inferred from the passage because the passage does not share statistics regarding the commonality of sex trafficking or labor trafficking. The passages states that labor trafficking victims are typically guarded with information regarding their employment and not willing to share information, unlike what choice B states. According to the passage, labor trafficking occurs in plain sight, not "behind closed doors" like choice D suggests.

80. A: Based on the passage, the most accurate statement is that a trafficking victim will likely not be able to provide any documentation regarding their identity. Many traffickers keep their victims' documents in an effort to control the victims' movements. They are also known to transport their victims to and from the work environment to further maintain that control, so choice C is incorrect. Victims of trafficking are not free to do as they wish outside of work hours like choice B suggests, nor are they free to leave the environment like choice D states, as they are highly controlled by traffickers.

81. C: Based on the passage, the most accurate statement is that being proactive is a key component to community policing. The passage explains that this approach leads to an overall decrease in crime and is more effective in doing so than traditional approaches, in contrast to what choice A states. There is no mention of a relationship between members of the community and how this could impact their relationship, so the statement in choice B cannot be inferred. It is also not suggested or stated that community members select the officers that will work in their neighborhoods like choice D suggests.

82. B: Based on the passage, the most accurate statement is that relationships are a pillar in community policing. The passage repeatedly highlights the importance and impact of relationships between officers and community members. The passage discusses a decrease in crime, but it links it to community policing strategies rather than increased patrol, contrary to what choice A argues. Choice C is incorrect because there is no mention of officers in community policing being held to different standards than those in traditional policing. Community members are able to work with police to develop strategies using this policing model, unlike what choice D suggests.

Cloze

83	What	**93**	away	**103**	of	**113**	that
84	the	**94**	at	**104**	least	**114**	minutes
85	speed	**95**	but	**105**	could	**115**	as
86	hour	**96**	car	**106**	that	**116**	His
87	Johnson	**97**	was	**107**	for	**117**	To
88	on	**98**	up	**108**	through	**118**	stop
89	first	**99**	when	**109**	calls	**119**	hands
90	road	**100**	off	**110**	being	**120**	car
91	stop	**101**	to	**111**	his	**121**	from
92	and	**102**	Should	**112**	as	**122**	during

Reasoning

123. A: The word *glad* is not like the other three. *Well, happily,* and *quickly* are all adverbs, which means they are used to describe verbs. *Glad* is an adjective. Well can also act as an adjective, but glad is the only choice that can only act as an adjective.

124. B: The next number in the sequence is 18. In this pattern, the numbers increase every time, but the amount of increase alternates between two and three.

125. C: Gertrude is the oldest. One way to solve a problem of this type is to assign an arbitrary age to the first person and then determine the rest of the ages relative to that one. So, if Denise is ten months old, then Ellen is seven months old, Francesca is nine months old, and Gertrude is thirteen months old.

126. A: The next number in the sequence is 4. This is a recurring pattern of three numbers: 4, 6, and 8. After 8, the pattern begins again with 4.

127. D: There is not enough information to solve this problem. The prompt provides information about the order of their ages, but since no specific ages are given, it is impossible to calculate Mary's age.

128. A: The word *Colombia* is not like the other three. *Connecticut, Delaware,* and *Wyoming* are all names of states, while *Colombia* is the name of a country.

129. B: The next number in the sequence is 727. In this sequence, each successive number has the digits shift forward one place, with the first digit becoming the last. Therefore, 772 would be followed by 727.

130. C: Erma ate six pies. If Doris ate seven pies, and Francine ate four fewer, then Francine ate three. If Erma ate three more pies than Francine, then she ate six.

131. D: There is not enough information to answer this question. It is clear that Jamal got the highest score, and that Lindsay got a higher score than Soo Yin, but it cannot be determined whether Lindsay or Bert had a higher score.

Practice Test #3

Clarity

Instructions: In the following pairs of sentences, identify the sentence that is most clearly written. If sentence "a" is clearer than sentence "b," mark "a" on your answer sheet. If sentence "b" is clearer than sentence "a," mark "b" on your answer sheet.

1.

a. Social scientists continue to debate the connection between crime and violent imagery in video games and movies.
b. Social scientists continue to debate the connection between crime plus violent imagery in video games and movies.

2.

a. There are a number of open desks for new recruits along the back wall of the room.
b. Along the back wall of the room, there are a number of open desks for new recruits.

3.

a. The police commissioner claimed that the conflicting information made it impossible for her to decide.
b. The police commissioner claimed that the conflicting information made it impossible for her to come to a decision.

4.

a. Even though both Sterling and Fred are in the choir, he has a much better voice.
b. Though Sterling and Fred are both in the choir, Sterling has a much better voice.

5.

a. As the victim drove home on Denver Boulevard, she was forced to the side of the road by another car.
b. The victim drove home, down Denver Boulevard, when she was forced to the side of the road by another car.

6.

a. The investigative work performed by Chandra was much better than any other detective.
b. The investigative work performed by Chandra was much better than that of any other detective.

7.

a. A productive day not only will include hard work but also will include rest and relaxation.
b. A productive day not only will include hard work and also will include rest and relaxation.

8.

a. Kevin spent most of his time reading magazines, playing video games, and taking naps.
b. Kevin spent most of his time reading magazines, playing video games, and take naps.

9.

a. The group of women she met for coffee occasionally asked her about her haircut.
b. The group of women she occasionally met for coffee asked her about her haircut.

10.

a. The actions you are suggesting would be in violation of the established rules.
b. The actions you are suggesting would violate the established rules.

11.

a. Driving to the crime scene, the car began to emit thick, black smoke.
b. The car began to emit thick, black smoke while he was driving to the crime scene.

12.

a. Frank had lived there all his life, yet he did not know the suspect.
b. Even though Frank had lived there all his life, yet he did not know the suspect.

13.

a. One of the students feels that the rules that apply to the class are too strict.
b. One of the students feel that the rules that apply to the class are too strict.

14.

a. Many of the calls came from citizens who the officers knew personally or worked near the police station.
b. Many of the calls came from citizens who the officers knew personally or who worked near the police station.

15.

a. During John's first lesson, the teacher asked him if he had any experience or if he ever read about famous artists.
b. During John's first lesson, the teacher asked him if he had any experience and did he ever read about famous artists.

16.

a. They checked the suspect's trunk, glove compartment, and center console before finding anything.
b. They checked the suspect's trunk, glove compartment, and his center console before finding anything.

17.

a. Officers take physical fitness tests. To demonstrate their abilities.
b. Officers take physical fitness tests to demonstrate their abilities.

18.

a. While he was running after the suspect, the officer understood why they did so many cardio exercises in the gym.
b. While he was running after the suspect, the officer understands why they did so many cardio exercises in the gym.

Spelling

Instructions: In the following sentences, choose the correct spelling of the missing word.

19. After it had a few weeks to heal, the scar on Stan's wrist was barely _______.

a. nodicable
b. notissable
c. noticable
d. noticeable

20. A quick search of the trunk established that the driver was in _______ of a large amount of contraband.

a. posesion
b. possession
c. possesion
d. posession

21. Felicia spent most of her time in the _______ reading about history and science.

a. library
b. liberry
c. librerry
d. librery

22. He declared that he would not sleep _______ the mess was totally cleaned up.

a. antill
b. until
c. untill
d. antil

23. Before Nell could see the doctor, she had to fill out a brief _______ about her medical history.

a. questionerre
b. questionnaire
c. questonairre
d. questionarre

24. Denise asked the clerk if there were any books she would _______ for a week at the beach.

a. recommend
b. reccomend
c. recommennd
d. recomend

25. He was very familiar with the risks of opening a new _______.

a. resterant
b. resturant
c. restaurant
d. restarrant

26. Daily ________ is one of the cornerstones of a healthy lifestyle and a generally positive mood.

a. exsercise
b. excercise
c. exercise
d. exorcise

27. There was plenty that Quincy wanted to say, but instead he held his ________.

a. tongue
b. tung
c. tonge
d. tungue

28. The food was good, but the tiny portions could not help but ________ the starving customers.

a. disappoint
b. dissapoint
c. disapoint
d. dessapoint

29. It was determined that the rock slide was only ________ related to the recent blizzard.

a. incedentally
b. incidentally
c. incidently
d. incidenatally

30. After tearing failed to work, Owen finally had to use ________ to remove the tag from his new sweater.

a. sizzers
b. sissors
c. scissors
d. scisors

31. For Lonnie, even getting bailed out by his ex-wife was ________ to another night in the county jail.

a. prefarable
b. preferable
c. prefferable
d. preferrable

32. Because he had never lived in a city, his ________ parking skills were undeveloped.

a. parallel
b. paralel
c. parulell
d. perralel

33. After a ________ review of the case files, the detective decided that several of the initial leads had been handled poorly.

a. through
b. thorough
c. thorow
d. thurrow

34. It is ________ to wear a Kevlar vest when responding to all calls.

a. necessary
b. necesary
c. neccesary
d. neccessary

35. Restraints had to be used on the ________ suspect for the safety of the officers.

a. agressive
b. aggressive
c. aggresive
d. aggrissive

36. Prison ________ play an important role in keeping inmates safe.

a. gards
b. gareds
c. guards
d. gauards

Vocabulary

Instructions: In each of the following sentences, choose the word or phrase that most nearly has the same meaning as the underlined word.

37. A coherent story would have helped his chances better than the stream of nonsense he provided.

a. Plausible
b. Frantic
c. Convincing
d. Understandable

38. In an organization with poor morale, employees may try to subvert the goals of their managers.

a. Support
b. Undermine
c. Freshen
d. Embolden

39. Viola felt there was no way to get the information she needed and not protract the conversation further.

a. Deliver
b. Enfold
c. Extend
d. Contend

40. Prunella did not see the cookies get taken, but she believed she could identify the culprit.

a. Fool
b. Humanitarian
c. Perpetrator
d. Breakfast

41. Darrel was allowed to remain on the scene so long as he did not interfere with the investigation.

a. Meddle
b. Confer
c. Delegate
d. Fend off

42. Despite the abundant trout in the river, Lorenzo and his son went all afternoon without even a bite.

a. Extreme
b. Plentiful
c. Improper
d. Collected

43. Instead of issuing a jail sentence, the judge elected to <u>levy</u> a strong fine against the offender.

a. Deny
b. Flag
c. Tariff
d. Impose

44. He hoped that his long apology would <u>appease</u> the disgruntled shopkeeper.

a. Anger
b. Satisfy
c. Conquer
d. Model

45. Loretta's <u>amiable</u> personality kept her from getting into too much trouble with her parents.

a. Possessive
b. Qualified
c. Friendly
d. Pugnacious

46. The size of the offer almost persuaded him to <u>forsake</u> the family business and move to the big city.

a. Betray
b. Ignore
c. Impersonate
d. Contain

47. He has a warm heart and can express <u>empathy</u> for even the most immoral offenders.

a. Criticism
b. Compassion
c. Collaboration
d. Extension

48. He was worried at first, because he knew they could never <u>duplicate</u> their amazing performance in the first match.

a. Fragment
b. Replicate
c. Detach
d. Demonstrate

49. Aaron tried to be <u>punctual</u>, but he always underestimated how long it would take him to get across town.

a. Timely
b. Slight
c. Delayed
d. Minor

50. Brenda felt a great deal of <u>animosity</u> towards her coworkers after they blamed her for the mishap.

a. Concern
b. Cooperation
c. Hatred
d. Contentment

51. He wrote down a list of facts he could use to <u>rebut</u> the arguments made against him.

a. Confirm
b. Disprove
c. Detail
d. Anticipate

52. It was discovered that the new software was <u>vulnerable</u> to cyberattacks.

a. Distant
b. Exposed
c. Capable
d. Prepared

53. No amount of jail time or community service would <u>rectify</u> what the felon had done.

a. Implicate
b. Remedy
c. Complete
d. Fulfill

54. The suspect seemed to <u>withdraw</u> from his friend group before the crimes were committed.

a. Disengage
b. Involve
c. Steal
d. Comply

Reading Comprehension

Refer to the following for questions 55–56:

Crime does not occur evenly over the landscape. It is clustered in small areas, or hot spots, that account for a disproportionate amount of crime and disorder. For example, in Minneapolis, 3% of the city's addresses accounted for 50% of calls for service to the police in one study. In Jersey City, NJ, about 4% of streets and intersection areas generated nearly half of the city's narcotics arrests and almost 42% of the disorder arrests. In addition to location, crime and public disorder tend to concentrate at certain times of the day or week. Assaults, for example, occur most frequently between 3:00 a.m. and 7:00 a.m., when streets are largely vacant. Residential burglaries mostly occur during daytime hours, when residents are not home. Incidents of driving under the influence occur more frequently in areas with a large number of bars or liquor stores.

55. Based on the preceding passage, which of the following statements is most accurate?

a. Crime tends to occur more often in particular areas.
b. Incidents of driving under the influence are more common along main roads.
c. Minneapolis police have ignored much of the city.
d. Residential burglaries usually occur during the night.

56. Based on the preceding passage, which of the following statements is most accurate?

a. Police should open stations in hot spots.
b. Public disorder usually occurs between three and seven in the morning.
c. Assaults are more likely to occur in populated areas.
d. Some times and places require more attention from police.

Refer to the following for questions 57–58:

Radio code is the coding system for identifying units both inside and outside the department. There are three components to every radio code. Each of these components must be included when officers are dispatched. In this coding system, units are identified with three characters: a letter designating the event, a number designating the level of emergency, and a number identifying the area.

Event	***Level of emergency***	***Area***
A: Domestic dispute	1: Emergency	1: Shackleford Banks
B: Burglary	2: Urgent	2: Financial District
C: Drug offense	3: Non-urgent	3: Sloan Street
D: Assault		4: Little Italy
E: Harassment		5: Government Plaza
F: Public intoxication		6: Morningside Heights
G: Traffic violation		7: Ashford Terrace
H: Disorderly conduct		

57. Using the above coding system, the call number F-2-1 would signify:

a. An urgent public intoxication incident at Shackleford Banks
b. An assault emergency on Sloan Street
c. A non-urgent traffic violation on Morningside Heights
d. A non-urgent traffic violation in the Financial District

58. Using the above coding system, the call number B-2-5 would signify:

a. An urgent burglary incident at Government Plaza
b. A public intoxication emergency on Sloan Street
c. An urgent disorderly conduct incident in Little Italy
d. A harassment emergency at Ashford Terrace

Refer to the following for question 59:

Police often ask eyewitnesses to identify a suspect from a lineup or an array of photos. A lineup or photo array involves placing a suspect or a photo of a suspect among people who are not suspected of committing the crime (fillers) and asking the eyewitness to identify the perpetrator. Misidentification by eyewitnesses has played a role in a high number of wrongful convictions and has led criminal justice experts to look more closely at the effectiveness of identifying suspects from live and photographic lineups.

59. Based on the preceding passage, which of the following statements is most accurate?

a. A photo array may contain only people who are not suspected of committing the crime.
b. The effectiveness of police lineups has been called into question recently.
c. A filler may have committed the crime.
d. The perpetrator will be asked to identify the criminal from a lineup.

Refer to the following for question 60:

When deciding to use less-lethal equipment, officers consider the circumstances and their agency's policy. Almost all larger law enforcement agencies have written policies about the use of less-lethal force. As part of their policy, agencies often have an approved use-of-force continuum to help officers decide the suitable amount of force for a situation—higher levels of force in the most severe circumstances, and less force in other circumstances. Many agencies in which officers use less-lethal technologies have training programs to help evaluate dangerous circumstances.

60. Based on the preceding passage, which of the following statements is most accurate?

a. Law enforcement agencies should give their officers clear instructions about the appropriate level of force for different situations.
b. The decision to use less-lethal equipment is entirely left to the officer on the scene.
c. Every law enforcement agency has a written policy about the use of less-lethal force.
d. Less-lethal force should be used in the most dangerous situations.

Refer to the following for question 61:

Investigators often need to examine or verify the authenticity of a document that could be used as evidence in court or as aid in an investigation. Such documents are known as "questioned documents." Through visual examination or advanced chemical analysis of inks and paper, forensic investigators can determine information relating to a questioned document's authentication, authorship, or creation date. Such documents, printed or handwritten, could include checks, criminal confessions, counterfeit money, journal entries, threatening letters, or wills.

61. Based on the preceding passage, which of the following statements is most accurate?

a. Most questioned documents are forged.
b. A questioned document must be authenticated before it can be used legally.
c. The authentication of questioned documents can take years.
d. A questioned document can never be fully authenticated.

Refer to the following for questions 62–63:

Racial profiling by law enforcement is commonly defined as a practice that targets people for suspicion of crime based on their race, ethnicity, religion, or national origin. Creating a profile about the kinds of people who commit certain types of crimes may lead officers to generalize about a particular group and act according to the generalization rather than specific behavior.

Racial profiling can cause multiple problems. Several law enforcement agencies have gone through expensive litigation over civil rights concerns. Police-citizen relations in those communities have been strained, making policing all the more challenging. Most important, racial profiling is unlikely to be an effective policing strategy, as criminals can simply shift their activities outside the profile (e.g., if racial profiling begins with police stopping black males in their teens and twenties for being drug carriers, criminals may start using other demographic groups—such as Hispanics, children, or the elderly—to move drugs). Despite training to avoid discrimination, officers may still rely on cultural stereotypes and act on their perceptions of a person's characteristics (such as age, race, or gender).

62. Based on the preceding passage, which of the following statements is most accurate?

a. The elderly are often the targets of racial profiling.
b. Racial profiling only applies to African Americans.
c. The worst consequence of racial profiling is expensive litigation for law enforcement departments.
d. Racial profiling may prevent a police officer from properly assessing a situation.

63. Based on the preceding passage, which of the following statements is most accurate?

a. Racial profiling is more common in diverse areas.
b. Anti-discrimination training has not been able to totally eradicate racial profiling.
c. Criminals cannot adapt to racial profiling.
d. Racial profiling is based on statistical data.

Refer to the following for question 64:

Social disorganization theory suggests that crime occurs when community relationships and local institutions fail or are absent. For example, a neighborhood with high residential turnover might have more crime than a neighborhood with a stable residential community.

64. Based on the preceding passage, which of the following statements is most accurate?

a. Social disorganization theory would likely recommend efforts to improve community relationships.
b. Social disorganization theory does not apply to urban areas.
c. Social disorganization theory places the responsibility for crime on residents.
d. Social disorganization theory has been proven false.

Refer to the following for questions 65–66:

Federal legislation allows U.S. Attorneys to enhance the penalty for crimes committed by gang members. A growing number of states have passed or are considering passing similar enhanced prosecution legislation. In practice, it is challenging to prove that an offender is a member of a gang or that the crime benefits the gang; therefore, it can be difficult to bring enhancement to bear on prosecuting criminal activity.

California, which leads the nation in the trend to enhance prosecution, describes the process this way: "any person who is convicted of a felony committed for the benefit of, at the direction of, or in association with any criminal street gang, with the specific intent to promote, further, or assist in any criminal conduct by gang members, shall, upon conviction of that felony, in addition and consecutive to the punishment prescribed for the felony," become subject to additional terms, enumerated in the code. Guidance is provided under the California code for persons convicted of misdemeanor offenses.

65. Based on the preceding passage, which of the following statements is most accurate?

a. Only states can enhance penalties because of gang membership.
b. Enhanced prosecution for gang members requires proof of gang membership.
c. Only California has passed enhanced prosecution legislation.
d. There are separate enhanced prosecution laws for repeat offenders.

66. Based on the preceding passage, which of the following statements is most accurate?

a. Crimes associated with gang activity are subject to harsher penalties in California.
b. Enhanced prosecution laws may apply to acts that are contrary to the gang's interests.
c. Misdemeanors are not subject to enhanced prosecution in California.
d. Gang members who commit crimes unrelated to their gang's activity may still be subject to enhanced prosecution.

Refer to the following for questions 67–68:

Stalking can be carried out in person or via electronic mechanisms (phone, fax, GPS, cameras, computer spyware, or the Internet). **Cyberstalking**—the use of technology to stalk victims—shares some characteristics with real-life stalking. It involves the pursuit, harassment, or contact of others in an unsolicited fashion initially via the Internet and email. Cyberstalking can intensify in chat rooms, where stalkers systematically flood their target's inbox with obscene, hateful, or threatening messages and images. A cyberstalker may further assume the identity of his or her victim by posting information (fictitious or not) and soliciting responses from the cybercommunity. Cyberstalkers may use information acquired online to further intimidate, harass, and threaten their victim via mail, phone calls, and physically appearing at a residence or workplace.

67. Based on the preceding passage, which of the following statements is most accurate?

a. Cyberstalking may include impersonating the victim.
b. Cyberstalking is identical to real-life stalking.
c. Cyberstalking is the most common form of stalking at present.
d. Cyberstalking rarely leads to real-life stalking.

68. Based on the preceding passage, which of the following statements is most accurate?

a. Cyberstalking is primarily perpetrated by women.
b. Episodes of cyberstalking are usually initiated by the victim.
c. Cyberstalking is unsolicited by the victim.
d. There is no connection between cyberstalking and other forms of stalking.

Refer to the following for questions 69–70:

Restorative justice principles offer more inclusive processes and reorient the goals of justice. Restorative justice has been finding a receptive audience, as it creates common ground that accommodates the goals of many constituencies and provides a collective focus. The guiding principles of restorative justice are:

1. Crime is an offense against human relationships.
2. Victims and the community are central to justice processes.
3. The first priority of justice processes is to assist victims.
4. The second priority is to restore the community, to the degree possible.
5. The offender has personal responsibility to victims and to the community for crimes committed.
6. Stakeholders share responsibilities for restorative justice through partnerships for action.
7. The offender will develop improved competency and understanding as a result of the restorative justice experience.

69. Based on the preceding passage, which of the following statements is most accurate?

a. Restorative justice is based on a close reading of the Constitution.
b. The first priority in justice is to arrest criminals, according to the restorative justice model.
c. In the restorative justice model, criminals should get nothing out of the process of justice.
d. Restorative justice suggests that offenders owe something to the community.

70. Based on the preceding passage, which of the following statements is most accurate?

a. Restorative justice requires the cooperation of all parties concerned.
b. Restorative justice is most appropriate for juvenile offenders.
c. The restorative justice model promotes changes in the sentencing process.
d. Restorative justice focuses on criminal rehabilitation.

Refer to the following for questions 71–72:

The political turmoil of the twenty-first century and advances in technology make transnational crime a concern for the United States. Increased travel and trade and advances in telecommunications and computer technology have had the unintended effect of providing avenues for the rapid expansion of transnational organized crime activities. Policing objectives in the United States must extend beyond national borders to seek out and target this type of crime. Only through international collaboration and information exchange can the United States develop effective protocol and policies for countering these crimes and mount a serious opposition.

71. Based on the preceding passage, which of the following statements is most accurate?

a. Transnational crime only occurs within the United States.
b. Transnational crime is more prevalent than domestic crime.
c. There should be an international organization for fighting transnational crime.
d. The rise of transnational crime has been fueled by the Internet.

72. Based on the preceding passage, which of the following statements is most accurate?

a. Advances in computer technology have benefited criminal organizations only.
b. The United States will need the help of other nations in fighting transnational crime.
c. The United States currently has an effective system for fighting transnational crime.
d. Transnational crime could be eliminated by stricter customs enforcement.

Refer to the following for questions 73–74:

Fraud is the intentional misrepresentation of information or identity to deceive others, the unlawful use of a credit or debit card or ATM, or the use of electronic means to transmit deceptive information, in order to obtain money or other things of value. Fraud may be committed by someone inside or outside a business. Fraud includes instances in which a computer was used to defraud the business of money, property, financial documents, insurance policies, deeds, use of rental cars, or various services by forgery, misrepresented identity, or credit card or wire fraud. The legal definition of fraud excludes incidents of embezzlement.

73. Based on the preceding passage, which of the following statements is most accurate?

a. Fraud is committed to obtain things of value.
b. Fraud can only be committed by an employee.
c. Today, most fraud involves the use of a computer.
d. The owner of a business cannot commit fraud.

74. Based on the preceding passage, which of the following statements is most accurate?

a. Most fraud involves the use of an ATM.
b. Unintentional deception can still be prosecuted as fraud.
c. Embezzlement is not considered fraud under the definition of the law.
d. Forgery is the most common form of fraud.

Refer to the following for questions 75–76:

Reducing the public's access to illicit substances is a large responsibility for law enforcement. There are three strategies police typically use when investigating drug trafficking cases with the goal of apprehending the trafficker. Witnessing a drug deal, also known as a hand-to-hand sale, in the streets is the lowest-level strategy. In this case, the dealer is instantly guilty of drug trafficking. If the buyer has purchased enough that it is clear they intend to distribute it, they may also face trafficking charges. In such cases, officers will need to testify to what they witnessed. Surveilling suspected dealers is another strategy. This is time-consuming and is typically reserved for major cases; it allows officers to collect first-hand information and insight over time. The last strategy is using informants or undercover officers. Informants provide information about drug traffickers to police, usually in exchange for immunity or leniency on charges they are facing. Informants are typically used in a controlled or observed sale. In controlled sales, officers give the informant money and send him or her to make a transaction. The informant then returns with the drugs and no money, confirming the drugs were purchased from the trafficker with whom the sale was arranged. As the name suggests, observed sales are witnessed by officers. In observed sales, the informant purchases drugs from a trafficker within view of the officer. When an undercover officer participates in the sale, it is called a direct sale.

75. Based on the preceding passage, which of the following statements is most accurate?

a. Controlled sales allow officers to watch a drug deal take place.
b. There are three sale strategies to implement when working with an informant.
c. Direct sales involve undercover officers participating in drug deals.
d. A sale to an informant can grant a trafficker leniency.

76. Based on the preceding passage, which of the following statements is most accurate?

a. Dealers in hand-to-hand sales are guilty of trafficking.
b. Most apprehensions are made as a result of surveillance.
c. A police officer witnessing a hand-to-hand drug deal is synonymous with an observed drug deal.
d. Undercover officers are responsible for observing informant drug deals.

Refer to the following for questions 77–78:

Hate crimes are criminal offenses motivated by prejudice toward marginalized groups, such as ethnic minorities, members of the LGBTQ community, and members of particular religions. These crimes are often committed to spark fear in victims and their communities. They sometimes escalate into hostile, dangerous incidents. As such, it is important that police response is swift. Once an officer has responded, secured the scene, and ensured the safety of all parties, he or she should work to preserve the crime scene by collecting and photographing any physical evidence and begin the preliminary investigation. The preliminary investigation will be conducted to obtain the identity of all involved, collect the suspect and witness statements, and make arrests if there is probable cause. Where possible, the victim should be interviewed by only one officer to avoid having to repeatedly retell traumatic experiences. An interpreter may be needed at this point in the investigation. In some instances, reports will need to be made to state or federal departments, depending on the crime. A follow-up investigation will occur in which officers continue to investigate and collect evidence, canvass for witnesses, and locate any offenders not arrested at the scene. Information collected should be shared with departments in the surrounding area to identify any patterns or trends in crimes and detect any organization involved. It is possible the media will report on the crime, so the information should be shared with a public information officer who can relay accurate and appropriate information about the crime to the media. The victim should also be made aware that they may see their case being discussed on news outlets.

77. Based on the preceding passage, which of the following statements is most accurate?

a. The investigation is completed once the offender has been arrested and the victim has been interviewed.
b. The victim should be interviewed as soon as the scene is secured.
c. Some hate crimes need to be documented federally.
d. Arrests are always made in the preliminary investigation.

78. Based on the preceding passage, which of the following statements is most accurate?

a. Public information officers should be the point of contact for media outlets.
b. Preserving the crime scene is a secondary responsibility for officers.
c. Victims should expect to recount their experience for multiple statements.
d. Offenders must be present on the scene in order to be arrested.

Refer to the following for questions 79–80:

Wellness checks, also sometimes referred to as welfare checks, occur when officers check in on someone at the request of a friend, acquaintance, or loved one. These checks can be initiated by calling 911 or the police non-emergency line, providing information about the individual that needs to be checked on, and having a valid reason for checking in. Valid reasons for checking in can include unreturned contact, suspicious activity around the person's home, or a suspected mental health crisis. Responding officers will first knock and announce their presence. If the person being checked on is found responsive and in good health, the police will contact the individual who made the call and inform him or her of their findings. If there is no response, officers will investigate around the home and check for signs that the person is in the home or in distress. They may ask neighbors for information on the individual they are checking on, such as when they last saw them and if they know their whereabouts. If no contact can be made, and officers are unable to establish a reason for the individual to not be home, they may forcefully enter the home. No warrant is needed if it is believed the individual's life is at risk. If the person being checked on is found in good health, officers will contact the individual who initiated the call and inform him or her. If the individual is found in distress, injured, or ill, officers will call for emergency medical assistance and then contact the individual who initiated the call. If the individual is found deceased, the caller will be informed, and police will launch an investigation into the cause of death.

79. Based on the preceding passage, which of the following statements is most accurate?

a. Officers must submit information that justifies them entering the home before doing so.
b. Officers will contact the individual who made the call regardless of the outcome.
c. Callers who initiate the wellness check must report to the home.
d. Officers do not need to wait for a response to enter the home.

80. Based on the preceding passage, which of the following statements is most accurate?

a. Officers are not expected to investigate the scene before entering.
b. Emergency medical personnel will assist officers in their initial response to welfare checks.
c. A caller must provide multiple reasons an individual needs to be checked on in order to initiate a welfare check.
d. If the individual is found well and the caller has been contacted, the officer's duties have been fulfilled.

Refer to the following for question 81:

When conducting long-term surveillance on a suspect, officers may utilize GPS tracking devices. Modern technology has made these devices smaller and, therefore, harder to detect. GPS trackers provide officers with constantly tracked data regarding the whereabouts of their suspects. This makes it easier to record a history of their activity and find their routines, and makes suspects easier to locate when it is time to make an arrest. Using devices to track is safer and more discreet than having officers tail their suspects. The only downfall is that if the devices are detected, they can be removed, destroyed, or affixed to a different vehicle.

81. Based on the preceding passage, which of the following statements is most accurate?

a. Once affixed, trackers cannot be removed by suspects.
b. Safety and discreetness are benefits of modern tracking devices.
c. Traditional surveillance methods are the most reliable methods.
d. Tracking devices only record data when requested by officers.

Refer to the following for question 82:

In situations where an officer has reasonable suspicion that an individual has committed, is about to commit, or is actively committing a crime, they can perform a stop-and-frisk. A stop-and-frisk is a brief pat-down of a suspect on the outside of their clothes to search for crime-related evidence. These are sometimes referred to as Terry stops. Any evidence found during a stop-and-frisk is admissible in court so long as the stop did not violate 4th Amendment rights that protect citizens from unreasonable searches and seizures.

82. Based on the preceding passage, which of the following statements is most accurate?

a. A stop-and-frisk does not violate a suspect's rights if performed correctly.
b. Officers are free to perform a stop-and-frisk on any person.
c. Only drugs are considered evidence in a stop-and-frisk.
d. Officers may request the suspect to remove outer layers of clothing during a stop-and-frisk.

Cloze

(83) _ _ _ _ _ 1974, it was believed that the maximum-security prison in Deloitte, Wisconsin was impossible (84) _ _ escape. However, in that (85) _ _ _ _, two cunning prisoners used a set of handmade tools to prove that (86) _ _ _ _ the best efforts of law enforcement could be undone (87) _ _ _ _ enough ingenuity, patience, and effort.

David Jackson and Fred Taylor had both been serving (88) _ _ _ _ sentences for murder in 1974. They were in the (89) _ _ _ _ cell block, and they also saw each other during their exercise time in (90) _ _ _ prison yard. Over their years together, (91) _ _ _ _ conceived of a plan to tunnel out of the prison through the (92) _ _ _ _ _ of the basement.

In order (93) _ _ _ this plan to work, however, the men needed to have a quality set of tools and regular access to the basement of the prison. Luckily for (94) _ _ _ _, the prison metal shop was located in the basement, and a few prisoners (95) _ _ _ _ allowed to work there as a reward for (96) _ _ _ _ behavior. Jackson and Taylor (97) _ _ _ _ sure to follow all of the prison rules, and within a few months, they were both able to secure jobs in the metal (98) _ _ _ _.

At that point, they (99) _ _ _ access to all of the tools they would need to cut a hole (100) _ _ _ _ _ _ _ the floor of the prison basement. However, they had to figure out a (101) _ _ _ to steal these tools so that the guards (102) _ _ _ _ _ _ _ know they were missing. Taylor was the one who (103) _ _ _ _ _ _ this problem. He figured (104) _ _ _ that by falsifying the metal shop's repair records, he could make it seem as (105) _ _ tools had broken and been discarded, (106) _ _ _ _ really they had been hidden elsewhere by Jackson and Taylor. Once the men had acquired enough tools to do the (107) _ _ _, they began slowly chipping away at the floor whenever they (108) _ _ _ a chance.

It took months for the two (109) _ _ _ to break through the cement floor, but once they had done this it appears that the work went much faster. They used shovels and pickaxes to (110) _ _ _ a tunnel under the northeastern wall of the prison complex, and they agreed to (111) _ _ _ _ until summer to escape because they believed that the denser foliage in the woods around the prison would make it easier for them to evade capture in the hours after the breakout.

Finally, on July 13, 1974, Jackson and Taylor (112) _ _ _ _ their move. They emerged from the ground about a hundred yards (113) _ _ _ _ the prison wall and immediately ran into the woods (114) _ _ _ _ _ they changed into a set of civilian clothes they had stolen months before. Their escape was not noticed by the authorities (115) _ _ _ _ _ four hours later.

The escape of David Jackson and Fred Taylor made the national newspapers (116) _ _ _ hugely embarrassed prison officials (117) _ _ _ had previously claimed that their facility was escape-proof. However, the story did not (118) _ _ _ happily for the two men. Jackson was apprehended two weeks (119) _ _ _ _ _ while trying to cross the border into Canada, and Taylor was gunned down (120) _ _ police outside his ex-wife's house five days after Jackson was captured. Still, this prison escape will go down in history as one of the (121) _ _ _ _ daring and unlikely in United (122) _ _ _ _ _ _ history.

Reasoning

Instructions: Officers often face situations in which they need to determine how different pieces of information relate to one another. In this section, you will be presented with information such as a group or ordered series of facts, numbers, letters, or words. Your task is to study the various pieces of information and try to understand how they relate to one another.

123. Identify the next number in the series: 12, 19, 26...

a. 31
b. 33
c. 35
d. 37

124. Three of the following words are similar, while one is different. Select the one that is different.

a. Elect
b. Candidate
c. Office-holder
d. Ballot

125. In the past year, Kevin made seven more arrests than Leonard, who made six more arrests than Mike. Nelson made ten more arrests than Mike. Who made the most arrests?

a. Kevin
b. Leonard
c. Mike
d. Nelson

126. Darren and Felix play in a basketball game. Darren scores three times as many points as Felix, who scores eight more than his average. How many points does Darren score?

a. 8
b. 9
c. 24
d. Not enough information

127. Identify the next number in the series: 7, 8, 9, 7, 8, 9, 7...

a. 7
b. 8
c. 9
d. 10

128. Three of the following things are similar, while one is different. Select the one that is different.

a. Fork
b. Spoon
c. Pan
d. Knife

129. Identify the next number in the series: 10, 21, 33, 46, 60...

a. 72
b. 73
c. 74
d. 75

130. Jake, Kevin, and Larry play on a basketball team. Jake scores 30 points, twice as many as Kevin. Larry scores 10 more points than Kevin. How many points did Larry score?

a. 10
b. 25
c. 40
d. Not enough information

131. Identify the next number in the series: 2, 5, 7, 8, 7, 5...

a. 0
b. 2
c. 5
d. 7

Answer Key and Explanations for Test #3

Clarity

1. A: In the other version, the conjunction *plus* is used incorrectly. The writer is describing a relationship between two different things: crime and violent imagery. The conjunction *plus* would lump these two things together, rather than keeping them separate so that they may be compared. In the correct version of the sentence, the terms are kept apart and the meaning is preserved.

2. B: The other version of the sentence suggests that the recruits, rather than the desks, are along the back wall of the room. By placing the location of the desks in an introductory clause, the correct version makes the location plain.

3. A: The other version of the sentence is unnecessarily wordy. The phrase "come to a decision" can be condensed to "decide" without changing the meaning.

4. B: The other version is unclear because it is hard to tell to whom *he* refers. One might suppose that it refers to Sterling, because he was mentioned first, but this cannot be guaranteed. The correct version substitutes the name for the pronoun *he*, and thus becomes clearer.

5. A: The other version of the sentence is grammatically correct, but it does not do a good job of emphasizing the most important information in the sentence: the attack on the victim. In the correct version of the sentence, the route taken by the victim is placed in an introductory subordinate clause, which encourages the reader to focus more on the information contained in the main clause. This is a subtle distinction, but a good writer will be able to draw the reader's attention to the most important parts of the text.

6. B: The other version of the sentence confuses the comparison. Because "that of" is omitted, it sounds as if Chandra's investigative work is better than the other detectives themselves rather than the work of those detectives. In the correct version, the terms of the comparison are clear.

7. A: In the other version, the conjunction *and* is used incorrectly. When the phrase "not only" is used at the beginning of a list (in this case, a list of the things included in a productive day), the second term in the list should be preceded by *but.*

8. A: In the other version, the verb tenses are inconsistent: *reading* and *playing* are gerunds (they end in *–ing*), while *take* is just in present tense.

9. B: In the other version, it cannot be determined whether she met the women occasionally or whether they occasionally asked her about her haircut. The correct version positions the adverb so that this meaning is clear.

10. B: The other version is too wordy. It is not necessary to write "would be in violation of" when "would violate" conveys the same meaning.

11. B: In the other version, it sounds as if the car was driving itself. Although a reader would most likely be able to make sense of this statement, the introductory clause creates unnecessary confusion. In the correct version, the driver is properly identified.

12. A: The other sentence is redundant. When the sentence begins with *even though*, it is not necessary to include yet as well. Another way to correct this sentence would be, "Even though Frank had lived there all his life, he did not know the suspect."

13. A: In the other version, the subject and verb disagree. The subject is singular (*one*) and the verb is plural (*feel*). Note that the subject is singular, even though it includes a plural noun (*students*).

14. B: In the other version of the sentence, it is unclear whether the officers or the citizens worked near the police station. Both of the items in the series should be introduced with the pronoun *who* in order for the meaning to be clear.

15. A: The other version of the sentence has an inconsistent structure. The sentence includes a list (things the teacher asked John about). In the correct version, every item in the list is introduced with *if*, while the incorrect version uses both *if* and *did* to introduce the items. The sentence is easier to read when the items in the list are introduced in the same way.

16. A: The possessive pronoun *his* is not necessary in this sentence. It is clear the center console belongs to the suspect without indicating it as his.

17. B: "To demonstrate their abilities" is a dependent clause, so it cannot stand on its own. It needs to be joined with the independent clause "officers take physical fitness tests."

18. A: Sentence B uses an incorrect verb tense. "While he was running" is past tense, so the verb in the following clause should also be past tense. This makes "understood" the correct choice, as it keeps the verb tenses the same.

Spelling

19. D: noticeable

20. B: possession

21. A: library

22. B: until

23. B: questionnaire

24. A: recommend

25. C: restaurant

26. C: exercise

27. A: tongue

28. A: disappoint

29. B: incidentally

30. C: scissors

31. B: preferable

32. A: parallel

33. B: thorough

34. A: necessary

35. B: aggressive

36. C: guards

Vocabulary

37. D: *Understandable* has the closest meaning to *coherent.* Both of them mean clear or easy to comprehend.

38. B: *Undermine* has the closest meaning to *subvert.* Both of these words mean to destroy or to rebel against authority.

39. C: *Extend* has the closest meaning to *protract.* Both of these words mean to make longer, whether in physical length or duration.

40. C: *Perpetrator* has the closest meaning to *culprit.* Both of these words refer to criminals or wrongdoers.

41. A: *Meddle* has the closest meaning to *interfere.* Both of these verbs mean to come between or to intervene.

42. B: *Plentiful* has the closest meaning to *abundant.* Both of them mean in great supply.

43. D: *Impose* has the closest meaning to *levy.* Both of these words mean apply or subject to.

44. B: *Satisfy* has the closest meaning to *appease.* Both of these words mean to make right or to give enough to.

45. C: *Friendly* has the closest meaning to *amiable.* Both of these words mean nice to other people or animals.

46. A: *Betray* has the closest meaning to *forsake.* Both of these verbs refer to acts of cruelty to supposed friends.

47. B: *Compassion* has the closest meaning to *empathy.* Both of these words mean concern or care for others.

48. B: *Replicate* has the closest meaning to *duplicate.* Both of these verbs mean to copy or mimic.

49. A: *Timely* has the closest meaning to *punctual.* Both of these words mean on time or exercising good timing.

50. C: *Hatred* has the closest meaning to *animosity.* Both of these words refer to anger towards another person.

51. B: *Disprove* has the closest meaning to *rebut.* Both of these words mean to argue against, contradict, or prove wrong.

52. B: *Exposed* has the closest meaning to *vulnerable.* Both words mean to be in danger or unprotected.

53. B: *Remedy* has the closest meaning to *rectify.* Both words mean to correct or make right.

54. A: *Disengage* has the closest meaning to *withdraw.* Both words mean to pull out of or leave.

Reading Comprehension

55. A: Based on the passage, the most accurate statement is that crime tends to occur more often in particular areas. According to the second sentence, "it is clustered in small areas." The passage states that incidents of driving under the influence are more common "in areas with a large number of bars or liquor stores," not along main roads. The passage never states that Minneapolis police ignored much of the city, only that their work was largely concentrated on a small number of places. Finally, the passage states that residential burglaries usually occur during daytime hours.

56. D: Based on the passage, the most accurate statement is that some times and places require more attention from police. These hot spots have been demonstrated to have more criminal activity. The passage does not, however, state that police should open stations in hot spots; there may be more effective ways to handle these problems. The passage states that assault, not public disorder, usually occurs between three and seven in the morning. In addition, assaults are more likely to occur when few other people are around.

57. A: Using the above coding system, the call number F-2-1 would signify an urgent public intoxication incident at Shackleford Banks.

58. A: Using the above coding system, the call number B-2-5 would signify an urgent burglary incident at Government Plaza.

59. B: Based on the passage, the most accurate statement is that the effectiveness of police lineups has been called into question recently. According to the final sentence, false convictions have undermined faith in traditional methods of identifying suspects. A photo array, meanwhile, will contain one suspect and several non-suspects, or fillers. These fillers are people who are not suspected of having committed the crime. Finally, the witness, and not the perpetrator, will be asked to identify the criminal from a lineup.

60. A: Based on the passage, the most accurate statement is that law enforcement agencies should give their officers clear instructions about the appropriate level of force for different situations. This is the main idea of the passage, and is expressed in every sentence. The decision about using less-lethal equipment is ideally a combination of the officer's assessment of the situation and the policy of the department. The passage states that "almost all larger law enforcement agencies have written policies," but clearly not all do. Finally, the passage states that officers will use "higher levels of force in the most severe circumstances, and less force in other circumstances."

61. B: Based on the passage, the most accurate statement is that a questioned document must be authenticated before it can be used legally. This is stated directly in the first sentence. Some questioned documents are forged, but the passage does not state that most are. The passage does not state that the authentication process can take years, or that it is impossible to ever fully authenticate a questioned document.

62. D: Based on the passage, the most accurate statement is that racial profiling may prevent a police officer from properly assessing a situation. The passage does not suggest that the elderly are often the targets of racial profiling, and indeed this would not really make sense. Similarly, there is no indication that racial profiling only applies to African Americans, though the passage does suggest that African Americans are subject to profiling. Expensive litigation may be a negative consequence of racial profiling, but it is by no means the worst.

63. B: Based on the passage, the most accurate statement is that anti-discrimination training has not been able to totally eradicate racial profiling. This fact is expressed in the final sentence of the passage. It seems possible that racial profiling is more common in diverse areas, but this is not expressed in the passage. The second paragraph describes how criminals will adapt quickly to racial profiling. Finally, the passage does not state that racial profiling is based on statistical data.

64. A: Based on the passage, the most accurate statement is that social disorganization theory would likely recommend efforts to improve community relationships. After all, this theory posits that poor relationships in the community contribute to increased crime. This theory clearly applies to urban areas and rural areas alike, and though it does suggest that the behavior of residents is an important factor in crime, the passage does not suggest that residents bear the responsibility. Finally, the passage does not indicate whether social disorganization theory has been accepted or proven false.

65. B: Based on the passage, the most accurate statement is that enhanced prosecution for gang members requires proof of gang membership. The first paragraph mentions that it can be difficult for attorneys to generate this proof. It is not true that only states can enhance prosecution; the first paragraph describes federal legislation that makes it possible for U.S. Attorneys to enhance interrogation. The second sentence of the first paragraph indicates that states besides California have passed enhanced prosecution legislation. The passage does not indicate that there are separate enhanced prosecution laws for repeat offenders.

66. A: Based on the passage, the most accurate statement is that crimes associated with gang activity are subject to harsher penalties in California. This is stated in the first sentence of the second paragraph. The passage makes clear that only acts that promote gang interests are subject to enhanced prosecution; in other words, unrelated crimes or crimes that are contrary to the gang's interests are not considered. The last sentence of the second paragraph indicates that misdemeanor offenses may also be subject to enhanced prosecution in California.

67. A: Based on the passage, the most accurate statement is that cyberstalking may include impersonating the victim. The passage states this directly: "A cyberstalker may further assume the identity of his or her victim..." The passage makes clear that cyberstalking "shares some characteristics with real-life stalking," but is not identical. The passage does not state that cyberstalking is the most common form of stalking at present, though it may be assumed that it is becoming more common. Finally, the passage does not indicate that cyberstalking rarely leads to real-life stalking; on the contrary, the final sentence suggests that this is not an uncommon occurrence.

68. C: Based on the passage, the most accurate statement is that cyberstalking is unsolicited by the victim. The third sentence states that cyberstalking "involves the pursuit, harassment, or contact of others in an unsolicited fashion." There is no suggestion that cyberstalking is primarily perpetrated by women. Furthermore, the passage does not indicate that most episodes of cyberstalking are initiated by the victim, though this also seems improbable. Finally, the passage makes plain in the second sentence that cyberstalking "shares some characteristics with real-life stalking."

69. D: Based on the passage, the most accurate statement is that restorative justice suggests that offenders owe something to the community. This is stated directly in the fifth item of the list. There is no suggestion in the passage that restorative justice is based on a close reading of the Constitution. The restorative justice model identifies assisting victims, not arresting criminals, as the first priority in restorative justice. Restorative justice does assert that the offender should develop "improved competency and understanding" out of the justice process.

70. A: Based on the passage, the most accurate statement is that restorative justice requires the cooperation of all parties concerned. This is clear in the sixth item of the list: "Stakeholders share responsibilities for restorative justice through partnerships for action." There is no indication that this model of justice is most appropriate for juvenile offenders, or that it promotes changes in the sentencing process. Criminal rehabilitation is part of the restorative justice model, but it is not necessarily the focus.

71. D: Based on the passage, the most accurate statement is that the rise of transnational crime has been fueled by the Internet. The passage suggests this in the first sentence ("advances in technology make transnational crime a concern") and further elaborates it in the second. Transnational crime, by definition, occurs across national borders. The passage does not state that transnational crime is more prevalent than domestic crime. The passage argues that there should be greater cooperation between nations in the fight against transnational crime, but does not state that there should be an international organization for fighting transnational crime.

72. B: Based on the passage, the most accurate statement is that the United States will need the help of other nations in fighting transnational crime. The final sentence states that "only through international collaboration" can the United States be effective in fighting these crimes. The passage does not state that advances in computer technology have benefited criminal organizations only, and it may be assumed that these advances have also aided investigation and prosecution efforts. It seems clear that the United States does not have an effective system for fighting transnational crime at present, and there is no indication in the passage that stricter customs enforcement could eliminate this problem.

73. A: Based on the passage, the most accurate statement is that fraud is committed to obtain things of value. The first sentence of the passage defines fraud as any of a number of deceptions committed "to obtain money or other things of value." The passage does not suggest that fraud can only be committed by an employee, and, indeed, it directly states that "fraud may be committed by someone inside or outside a business." The passage does not state that most fraud today involves the use of a computer, though it does indicate that computers are often used in fraud. Finally, the passage never states that the owner of a business cannot commit fraud. On the contrary, the definition of the crime suggests that it may be committed by any person in any position.

74. C: Based on the passage, the most accurate statement is that embezzlement is not considered fraud under the definition of the law. This is stated explicitly in the last sentence. The passage does not suggest that forgery is the most common form of fraud, or that most fraud involves the use of an ATM, though both of these scenarios are listed as forms of fraud. The passage states that fraud must be an intentional misrepresentation, so it would seem that unintentional deception could not be prosecuted as fraud.

75. C: Based on the passage, the most accurate statement is that direct sales involve undercover officers participating in drug deals. In direct sales, undercover officers purchase drugs directly from traffickers. There are three strategies outlined for investigating trafficking: witnessing sales, surveillance, and using informants or undercover officers. Contrary to what choice B suggests. there are only two types of sales when working with informants: controlled sales and observed sales. The passage explains that in controlled sales, money is given to the informant, who then purchases drugs. Choice A is incorrect because officers do not witness controlled sales like they do observed sales. The passage also explains that informants may be granted immunity or leniency for any charges they are facing, not the trafficker as choice D states.

76. A: Based on the passage, the most accurate statement is that dealers in hand-to-hand sales are guilty of trafficking. This is stated in the passage. It is explained that surveillance is not often used due to it being time-consuming; therefore, it is unlikely to account for the majority of apprehensions as choice B argues. Choice C is incorrect because a police officer witnessing a hand-to-hand drug deal is not the same as an observed drug deal. An observed deal involves an informant, while a hand-to-hand deal occurs between two suspects. The passage does not mention that undercover officers are responsible for witnessing informant deals, so choice D cannot be inferred.

77. C: Based on the passage, the most accurate statement is that some hate crimes need to be documented federally. The passage states that, in some instances, reports will need to be made to state or federal departments. The investigation is not considered complete after an arrest has been made and the victim has been interviewed like choice A suggests. Instead, officers must continue to collect evidence and look for witnesses, share information across departments, and potentially inform the media of new developments in the case after the offender has been arrested. Unlike what choice B argues, the victim should not be interviewed until a dedicated officer can complete the interview and, if necessary, an interpreter is available. Arrests are not always made in the preliminary investigation as choice D suggests because there must be probable cause.

78. A: Based on the passage, the most accurate statement is that public information officers should be the point of contact for media outlets. Information regarding the crime that can be made public should be shared with public information officers so that they can respond to media requests. Preserving the crime scene is one of the first things an officer does when they arrive, so it would not be considered a secondary responsibility as stated in choice B. The passage mentions that, ideally, the victim will only give their statement to one officer, so choice C is incorrect. The passage also explains that arrests can occur during the follow-up investigation—not only on the scene as choice D claims.

79. B: Based on the passage, the most accurate statement is that officers will contact the individual who made the call regardless of the outcome. In each scenario provided, it is stated that officers will inform the individual who requested the wellness check of the outcome. Choice A is incorrect because officers do not need to submit any information before entering the home if they believe someone's life is at risk. The passage does not state or suggest that the caller who initiated the check must report to the home like choice C states, only that he or she will be contacted. Officers should wait for a response after knocking before proceeding to enter, so choice D is incorrect.

80. D: Based on the passage, the most accurate statement is that if the individual is found to be well and the caller has been contacted, the officer's duties have been fulfilled. There is no need for any additional action by the officer. If officers do not get a response, they should investigate the scene for signs that the individual is currently in the dwelling, unlike what choice A suggests. Emergency medical personnel will only be called if the individual is found injured or ill. It is not stated that they are called to the scene otherwise, so choice B is incorrect. The passage lists a few reasons that can justify a welfare check, but it does not state that multiple must apply for a check to be conducted as stated in choice C.

81. B: Based on the passage, the most accurate statement is that safety and discreetness are benefits of modern tracking devices. The passage states that using these tools is safer and more discrete than having officers tail their suspects. Contrary to choice A, the passage states that the trackers can be removed and destroyed. Traditional surveillance methods are not more reliable like choice C argues because modern methods are harder to detect and record data at all times—not just when requested by officers like choice D claims.

82. A: Based on the passage, the most accurate statement is that a stop-and-frisk does not violate a suspect's rights if performed correctly. So long as there is reasonable suspicion that an individual has committed, is about to commit, or is actively committing a crime, a stop-and-frisk does not violate 4th Amendment rights. Officers can only perform this on individuals who meet those criteria, not any person they see in the street, so choice B is incorrect. Choice C is incorrect because any form of evidence may be collected during these stops. Pat-downs are only for the outer layer of clothing, and the passage does not state that officers can request suspects to remove clothes, so choice D is incorrect.

Cloze

83	Until	**93**	for	**103**	solved	**113**	from or past
84	to	**94**	them	**104**	out	**114**	where
85	year	**95**	were	**105**	if	**115**	until
86	even	**96**	good	**106**	when	**116**	and
87	with	**97**	were	**107**	job	**117**	who
88	life	**98**	shop	**108**	had	**118**	end
89	same	**99**	had	**109**	men	**119**	later
90	the	**100**	through	**110**	dig	**120**	by
91	they	**101**	way	**111**	wait	**121**	most
92	floor	**102**	wouldn't	**112**	made	**122**	States

Reasoning

123. B: The next number in the series is 33. In this series, the numbers increase by seven each time.

124. A: The word *elect* is not like the other three. *Candidate*, *office-holder*, and *ballot* are all nouns related to voting and democracy, while *elect* is a verb.

125. A: Kevin has made the most arrests. If Kevin made seven more arrests than Leonard, who made six more than Mike, then Kevin made thirteen more arrests than Mike. Therefore, Kevin also made three more arrests than Nelson.

126. C: There is not enough information to solve this problem. Felix's average point total is not given, so it is impossible to calculate Darren's point total for the game.

127. B: The next number in the series is 8. This pattern is just recurring groups of three numbers: 7, 8, and 9. So, after each 7 would come an 8.

128. C: A pan is not like the other three things. Forks, spoons, and knives are all eating utensils, but a pan is not.

129. D: The next number in the series is 75. The difference between the terms in this series increases by one with each successive term.

130. B: Larry scored 25 points. If Jake scored 30 points, and this was twice as many as Kevin, then Kevin scored 15. If Larry scored 10 more points than Kevin, then Larry must have scored 25 points.

131. B: The next number in the series is 2. This series is symmetrical; that is, it increases to 8 and then retraces its steps back down to 2.

Practice Test #4

Clarity

Instructions: In the following pairs of sentences, identify the sentence that is most clearly written. If sentence "a" is clearer than sentence "b," mark "a" on your answer sheet. If sentence "b" is clearer than sentence "a," mark "b" on your answer sheet.

1.

a. Pedro began his shift by filling his service vehicle with gas and a cup of coffee.
b. Pedro began his shift by filling his service vehicle with gas and buying a cup of coffee.

2.

a. The department budget is inflated now because of purchases like the new fax machine.
b. The department budget is inflated at this point in time because of purchases along the lines of the new fax machine.

3.

a. Receiving the diploma, his instructor called Leonard the best student he had ever had.
b. As Leonard received his diploma, his instructor called him his best student ever.

4.

a. He filled his notebook with interesting comments from the neighbors and onlookers while he was collecting evidence.
b. Collecting evidence, his notebook filled with interesting comments from the neighbors and onlookers.

5.

a. The guys he ran into in the locker room sometimes bragged about their fancy cars.
b. Sometimes, the guys he ran into in the locker room bragged about their fancy cars.

6.

a. Although the district is well funded overall, the police department lacks even the most basic supplies.
b. Although the district is well funded overall, but the police department lacks even the most basic supplies.

7.

a. The protesters resisted the police's efforts to subdue them.
b. The protesters were resistant to the police's efforts to subdue them.

8.

a. Citizens are advised to remain in their homes if possible until the situation has been resolved.
b. Until the situation has been resolved, citizens are advised to, if possible, remain in their homes.

9.

a. I was working at the library when I heard the news about Trevor's acquittal.
b. I was doing homework at the library when I heard the news about Trevor's acquittal.

10.

a. Just when he thought it was over, Lonnie remembers his training and returns to the crime scene.
b. Just when he thought it was over, Lonnie remembered his training and returned to the crime scene.

11.

a. An effective supervisor knows when to ignore minor errors.
b. An effective supervisor knows when they need to ignore minor errors.

12.

a. The correct procedure for detaining a suspect was second nature to Kelly after she completed the training course.
b. After completing the training course, the correct procedure for detaining a suspect was second nature to Kelly.

13.

a. Government oversight is where elected officials examine the policies and actions of city employees, including the police department.
b. Government oversight is the examination of the policies and actions of city employees, including the police department, by elected officials.

14.

a. The magazine journalists who cover law enforcement are much more fair-minded than the newspapers.
b. The magazine journalists who cover law enforcement are much more fair-minded than those of the newspapers.

15.

a. In the richest neighborhoods, all cars were not properly registered with the municipal department.
b. In the richest neighborhoods, not all cars were properly registered with the municipal department.

16.

a. The new officer said he wouldn't never break his oath.
b. The new officer said he wouldn't break his oath.

17.

a. The suspect exclaimed that he would stop running and to stop chasing him.
b. The suspect exclaimed that he would stop running and yelled to stop chasing him.

18.

a. It was a cold day out, he brought his thick jacket and gloves with him on patrol.
b. It was a cold day out, so he brought his thick jacket and gloves with him on patrol.

Spelling

Instructions: In the following sentences, choose the correct spelling of the missing word.

19. "I ________ wish things had gone differently," she said with obvious regret.

a. truely
b. truly
c. trooly
d. trewly

20. The officer responded to a frantic call from a citizen, but when she arrived, she found nothing more than some minor ________.

a. mischief
b. mischeff
c. mischiff
d. mischeif

21. Unless there is an immediate ________ in unnecessary spending, the project will be way over budget.

a. reduckshen
b. reduction
c. reducton
d. reducshen

22. His excellent performance in several subjects made him a natural ________ for the "Best All-Around Student" award.

a. cadidate
b. cannadate
c. candidate
d. cannidate

23. The mission would require a great deal of outdoor reconnaissance, so the team leader required all the soldiers to pack their ________ uniforms.

a. camelflage
b. camofladge
c. camouflage
d. camoflage

24. Frank did not break any bones in the accident, but his ________ was torn in several places.

a. cartilage
b. cartilege
c. carrtiladge
d. cartilige

25. The ________ story is that his car slipped out of gear and rolled downhill, but we all know that the truth is quite different.

a. offishel
b. official
c. offishul
d. offeshel

26. The printer offered a complete ________: if customers were not satisfied with the finished product, they could have their money back.

a. guarantee
b. garantee
c. garauntee
d. gaurantee

27. Once she learned how to operate the program, she began to ________ points at a steady pace.

a. acumulate
b. acummulate
c. accumulate
d. acumullate

28. She was looking forward to the end of the school year, when she could finally devote her full attention to developing her small ________.

a. busyness
b. bizzeness
c. bussiness
d. business

29. She loved coming home on the weekends, ________ when her brother and sister were in town as well.

a. especially
b. espeshelley
c. aspicially
d. especheIly

30. He was the first in his family to ________ in any sport, and his parents hardly knew how to react.

a. axel
b. excel
c. axul
d. axcel

31. Julian's background in ________ was a major advantage in his new laboratory job.

a. science
b. sience
c. siunce
d. scyence

32. She felt that she had run as well as she could, but she still only finished in ________ place.

a. furth
b. forth
c. fourth
d. fourfth

33. The situation was further complicated when it was discovered that the cans had not been ________ properly.

a. labeled
b. labelled
c. labiled
d. labeiled

34. Paperwork is organized by the ________ it fulfills.

a. category
b. catagory
c. catigory
d. catogory

35. The public relations officer acts as a ________ between the community and the department.

a. liason
b. laison
c. liaison
d. leasion

36. The sheriff won the election by a small ________.

a. margen
b. margon
c. margin
d. marggin

Vocabulary

Instructions: In each of the following sentences, choose the word or phrase that most nearly has the same meaning as the underlined word.

37. His harsh manner managed to aggravate most of his coworkers within a few weeks.

a. Irritate
b. Allow
c. Debate
d. Announce

38. To rectify his mistake, he pledged an annual donation to the school's scholarship fund.

a. Alter
b. Correct
c. Ensnare
d. Delay

39. He was terrified that the other children would humiliate him because of his stutter.

a. Conquer
b. Embarrass
c. Ease
d. Placate

40. His pyramid scheme was perfectly organized to bilk senior citizens out of their life savings.

a. Feel
b. Establish
c. Offend
d. Con

41. Though he remained supine, from the couch he ordered his bodyguards to show the visitor out immediately.

a. Recumbent
b. Relaxed
c. Entire
d. Attentive

42. During his descent from the peak, the change in air pressure began to make him nauseous.

a. Expensive
b. Injured
c. Improper
d. Lowering

43. He was able to surmount every obstacle along the way, from bad weather to inconsistent equipment.

a. Continue
b. Overcome
c. Express
d. Select

44. The plan to <u>allocate</u> the funds equally was complicated by the absence of several key committee members.

a. Distribute
b. Enrapture
c. Ruin
d. Hoard

45. His quest for <u>redemption</u> began by repairing the property he had damaged.

a. Collection
b. Fascination
c. Collapse
d. Recovery

46. They could never fully explain the <u>rationale</u> behind their decision to move.

a. Continue
b. Encourage
c. Finish
d. Reason

47. He didn't request <u>remuneration</u>, but he was happy to accept it when it was offered.

a. Assembly
b. Payment
c. Entrapment
d. Flow

48. His best efforts were not enough to <u>supplant</u> Hector at the top of the tennis rankings.

a. Replace
b. Send Out
c. Deny
d. Acknowledge

49. The <u>plaintiff</u> contended that Steve was behind the wheel when the mailbox was destroyed.

a. Subject
b. Container
c. Accuser
d. Declaration

50. He hoped to <u>incite</u> action with his impassioned speech.

a. Diminish
b. Encourage
c. Slant
d. Languish

51. The jury took only an hour before rendering its <u>decision</u>.

a. Address
b. Allowance
c. Summary
d. Verdict

52. The con artist was <u>cunning</u> and managed to steal thousands from his victims.

a. Shapely
b. Open
c. Proper
d. Clever

53. Training took place in a <u>simulated</u> active shooter situation.

a. Natural
b. Suspected
c. Imitation
d. Variable

54. The suspect was found <u>competent</u> to stand trial.

a. Capable
b. Inadequate
c. Hopeful
d. Happy

Reading Comprehension

Refer to the following for questions 55–56:

Geography has a major influence on crime. The features and characteristics of cityscapes and rural landscapes can make it easier or more difficult for crime to occur. The placement of alleys, buildings, and open spaces, for example, affects the likelihood that a criminal will strike. Combining geographic data with police report data and then displaying the information on a map is an effective way to analyze where, how, and why crime occurs.

Computerized crime maps became more commonplace with the introduction of desktop computing and software programs called geographic information systems (GIS). Analysts map where crime occurs, combine the resulting visual display with other geographic data (such as location of schools, parks, and industrial complexes), analyze and investigate the causes of crime, and develop responses. Recent advances in statistical analysis make it possible to add more geographic and social dimensions to the analysis.

55. Based on the preceding passage, which of the following statements is most accurate?

a. Geographical data is more useful in urban areas.
b. Criminals are more likely to strike in open areas.
c. Geographical data can be very useful in law enforcement.
d. Police report data is useless without geographical data.

56. Based on the preceding passage, which of the following statements is most accurate?

a. Police have only recently begun using geographical data in their work.
b. Technological innovation has further increased the utility of geographic data.
c. Geographic information systems have reduced the crime rate.
d. The causes of crime can all be attributed to geographic factors.

Refer to the following for questions 57–58:

It's a fact that certain kinds of activities can indicate terrorist plans that are in the works, especially when they occur at or near high-profile sites or places where large numbers of people gather—like government buildings, military facilities, utilities, bus or train stations, or major public events. If you see or know about suspicious activities, please report them immediately to the proper authorities. In the United States, that means your closest Joint Terrorism Task Force, located in an FBI field office. In other countries, that means your closest law enforcement/counterterrorism agency.

57. Based on the preceding passage, which of the following statements is most accurate?

a. Public assistance is needed in the fight against terrorism.
b. Other countries do not have effective counterterrorism organizations.
c. Terrorists are usually more interested in unpopulated areas.
d. Civilians should not be near military facilities under any circumstances.

58. Based on the preceding passage, which of the following statements is most accurate?

a. Every FBI field office contains a Joint Terrorism Task Force.
b. Some activities are more suspicious when they occur in particular places.
c. Citizens should attempt to apprehend terrorism suspects on their own.
d. A large number of people tend to gather at utility stations.

Refer to the following for questions 59–60:

Crime pattern theory integrates crime within a geographic context that demonstrates how the environments people live in and pass through influence criminality. The theory specifically focuses on places and the lack of social control or other measures of guardianship that are informally needed to control crime. For example, a suburban neighborhood can become a hot spot for burglaries because some homes have inadequate protection and nobody home to guard the property.

59. Based on the preceding passage, which of the following statements is most accurate?

a. Crime pattern theory is only concerned with suburban crime.
b. Crime pattern theory places the responsibility for crime on the neighborhood watch.
c. Crime pattern theory focuses on the relationship between crime and place.
d. Crime pattern theory applies only to minor offenses, like burglary.

60. Based on the preceding passage, which of the following statements is most accurate?

a. Social control can help mitigate crime.
b. Crime always occurs in areas with low social control.
c. A high degree of social control will prevent crime.
d. Society plays a larger role than law enforcement in stopping crime.

Refer to the following for questions 61–62:

One of the most common forms of evidence investigators may detect and collect at a crime scene is impression and pattern evidence.

Impression evidence is created when two objects come in contact with enough force to cause an "impression." Typically, impression evidence is either two-dimensional—such as a fingerprint—or three-dimensional—such as the marks on a bullet caused by the barrel of a firearm.

Pattern evidence may be additional identifiable information found within an impression. For example, an examiner will compare shoeprint evidence with several shoe-sole patterns to identify a particular brand, model, or size. If a shoe recovered from a suspect matches this initial pattern, the forensic examiner can look for unique characteristics that are common between the shoe and the shoeprint, such as tread wear, cuts, or nicks.

61. Based on the preceding passage, which of the following statements is most accurate?

a. Impression evidence is more valuable than pattern evidence.
b. Shoes are the most common source of pattern evidence.
c. A footprint on a carpet would be an example of impression evidence.
d. Pattern evidence must be verified by a state laboratory before it can be admitted for trial.

62. Based on the preceding passage, which of the following statements is most accurate?

a. Forensic examiners can match a shoe to a shoe print.
b. Pattern evidence requires less analysis than impression evidence.
c. A left shoe cannot be matched to a right shoe print.
d. A shoe print is not enough evidence to generate a conviction.

Refer to the following for question 63:

The **broken windows theory** explains how lesser crimes, untended areas, blight, graffiti, and signs of disorder decrease neighborhood residents' willingness to enforce social order, which in turn leads to more serious crime. If police target minor transgressions, they may prevent serious crime from developing in those places.

63. Based on the preceding passage, which of the following statements is most accurate?

a. The broken windows theory would explain crime in wealthy neighborhoods.
b. According to the broken windows theory, vandalism is the worst crime.
c. The broken windows theory does not apply to rural areas.
d. The broken windows theory draws a link between minor and major crimes.

Refer to the following for questions 64–65:

Current research finds that the management and culture of a department are the most important factors influencing police behavior. How the department is managed will dramatically affect how officers behave toward citizens. Additionally, how officers behave toward citizens will affect whether citizens view law enforcement as an institution with integrity.

Organizations that place priorities in the following areas will do better at maintaining integrity: accountability of managers and supervisors; equal treatment for all members of the organization; citizen accessibility to the department; inspections and audits; and quality education for employees. Defining values and principles and incorporating them in every facet of operations may be more important than hiring decisions. Diligence in detecting and addressing misconduct will show officers that managers practice what they preach.

64. Based on the preceding passage, which of the following statements is most accurate?

a. Departmental culture is separate from how officers interact with the public.
b. Law enforcement departments should get recommendations from citizens.
c. The primary factor influencing police behavior is the crime rate.
d. Departmental culture has far-reaching effects in law enforcement.

65. Based on the preceding passage, which of the following statements is most accurate?

a. An organization should have defined values and principles.
b. Once organizational policies are in place, managers should be able to ignore them.
c. Misconduct generally takes a long time to detect.
d. Managers will receive preferential treatment in effective organizations.

Refer to the following for questions 66–67:

Radio code is the coding system for identifying units both inside and outside the department. There are three components to every radio code. Each of these components must be included when officers are dispatched. In this coding system, units are identified with three characters: a letter designating the shift, a number designating the area, and a letter identifying the type of event.

Shift	*Area*	*Event*
A: Day	0: Central	A: Drug offense
B: Swing	1: South	B: Traffic violation
C: Graveyard	2: East	C: Disorderly conduct
	3: West	D: Assault
	4: North	E: Robbery
		F: Vandalism

66. Using the above coding system, the call number A-4-A would signify:

a. A drug offense in the northern part of the city during the day shift
b. A traffic violation in the southern part of the city during the swing shift
c. Disorderly conduct in the western part of the city during the graveyard shift
d. An assault in the southern part of the city during the day shift

67. Using the above coding system, the call number B-0-B would signify:

a. Disorderly conduct in the western part of the city during the graveyard shift
b. A traffic violation in the central part of the city during the swing shift
c. Harassment in the eastern part of the city during the day shift
d. An assault in the western part of the city during the swing shift

Refer to the following for question 68:

Transnational organized crime involves the planning and execution of illicit business ventures by groups or networks of individuals working in more than one country. These criminal groups use systematic violence and corruption to achieve their goals. Crimes commonly include money laundering, human smuggling, cybercrime, and trafficking of humans, drugs, weapons, endangered species, body parts, or nuclear material.

68. Based on the preceding passage, which of the following statements is most accurate?

a. Transnational crime often involves smuggling contraband across national borders.
b. Transnational crime is most common in Eastern Europe.
c. Transnational crime is restricted to the Internet.
d. Transnational crime is only a problem for the United States.

Refer to the following for question 69:

Evidence refers to information or objects that may be admitted into court for judges and juries to consider when hearing a case. Evidence can come from various sources, such as genetic material, trace chemicals, dental history, or fingerprints. Evidence can serve many roles in an investigation, such as to trace an illicit substance, identify remains, or reconstruct a crime.

69. Based on the preceding passage, which of the following statements is most accurate?

a. It is difficult to use dental history in a trial.
b. Evidence does not need to be admitted into court to be considered by a jury.
c. Only the prosecution may introduce evidence during a trial.
d. Evidence does not have to be physical material.

Refer to the following for question 70:

People between the ages of 15 and 24 are most likely to be targeted by gun violence as opposed to other forms of violence. From 1976 to 2005, 77% of homicide victims ages 15–17 died from gun-related injuries. This age group was most at risk for gun violence during this time period. Teens and young adults are more likely than persons of other ages to be murdered with a gun. Most violent gun crime, especially homicide, occurs in cities and urban communities.

70. Based on the preceding passage, which of the following statements is most accurate?

a. Young adults are more likely to commit acts of gun violence.
b. Teenagers and young adults are more likely than other people to be the victims of gun violence.
c. The leading cause of death among middle-aged citizens is not gun violence.
d. Most gun violence occurs in rural areas.

Refer to the following for question 71:

Enduring stress for a long period of time can lead to anxiety, depression, or post-traumatic stress disorder (PTSD). PTSD is a psychological condition marked by an inability to be intimate, inability to sleep, increased nightmares, increased feelings of guilt, and reliving the event. For law enforcement officers, stress can increase fatigue to the point that decision making is impaired and officers cannot properly protect themselves or citizens.

71. Based on the preceding passage, which of the following statements is most accurate?

a. Stress can be detrimental to an officer's performance.
b. PTSD is associated with excessive sleeping.
c. Most law enforcement officers suffer from fatigue.
d. Depression can lead to stress.

Refer to the following for questions 72–73:

Like domestic violence, stalking is a crime of power and control. Stalking is conservatively defined as "a course of conduct directed at a specific person that involves repeated (two or more occasions) visual or physical proximity, nonconsensual communication, or verbal, written, or implied threats, or a combination thereof, that would cause a reasonable person fear." Stalking behaviors also may include persistent patterns of leaving or sending the victim unwanted items or presents that may range from seemingly romantic to bizarre, following or lying in wait for the victim, damaging or threatening to damage the victim's property, defaming the victim's character, or harassing the victim via the Internet by posting personal information or spreading rumors about the victim.

72. Based on the preceding passage, which of the following statements is most accurate?

a. Stalking does not occur unless a person is intending to stalk.
b. Stalking and domestic violence are the same crime.
c. Stalking requires physical proximity.
d. Stalking must include multiple episodes.

73. Based on the preceding passage, which of the following statements is most accurate?

a. Stalking requires verbal communication.
b. Sending a person flowers could be part of a pattern of stalking.
c. Most stalking goes unreported by the victims.
d. Stalking may include physical violence against another person.

Refer to the following for questions 74–75:

Burglary is the unlawful or forcible entry or attempted entry of a residence. This crime usually, but not always, involves theft. The illegal entry may be by force, such as breaking a window or slashing a screen, or may be without force by entering through an unlocked door or an open window. As long as the person entering has no legal right to be present in the structure, a burglary has occurred.

Furthermore, the structure need not be the house itself for a burglary to take place; illegal entry of a garage, shed, or any other structure on the premises also constitutes household burglary. If breaking and entering occurs in a hotel or vacation residence, it is still classified as a burglary for the household whose member or members were staying there at the time the entry occurred.

74. Based on the preceding passage, which of the following statements is most accurate?

a. Burglary rarely occurs at vacation residences.
b. Burglary cannot occur at a hotel.
c. Burglary always occurs at a residence, even when that residence is not a home.
d. There are situations in which burglary is lawful.

75. Based on the preceding passage, which of the following statements is most accurate?

a. A burglar may have a legal right to the residence where the burglary occurs.
b. Burglary without force is better than burglary with force.
c. A burglary may be committed without a theft taking place.
d. Breaking into a shed is considered burglary regardless of where the shed is located.

Refer to the following for question 76:

Police officers can help to directly support schools by working as a school resource officer, also known as an SRO. SROs have the same powers and authority as other officers, such as responding to calls and making arrests, but they also work beyond that to serve as educators, mentors, and emergency managers in schools. They are the first line of defense in an active shooter situation or other situations in which the well-being of students is at risk.

76. Based on the preceding passage, which of the following statements is most accurate?

a. SROs do not interact directly with students.
b. SROs have some responsibilities beyond those of their peers.
c. SROs do not have the same authority as street cops.
d. SROs have less responsibility than their peers working outside of schools.

Refer to the following for question 77:

There will be scenarios in which officers must exceed safe driving speeds in order to apprehend suspects. When suspects fail to stop, high-speed chases can occur. Before engaging in a high-speed chase, an officer must determine if pursuit is necessary. Officers should consider what reasons exist for the chase, how important it is that the violator be stopped, what the violator has done, and who will be at risk during the chase. Officers must also consider their own driving abilities and confidence in pursuit when making their decision. Some departments do not allow officers to engage in chases, but for those that do, the decision is up to the responding officer. Officers who engage in a chase may stop pursuit if unsafe conditions develop. Alternatively, officers can request roadblocks along a suspect's route to help stop them without engaging in a high-speed chase.

77. Based on the preceding passage, which of the following statements is most accurate?

a. Once an officer begins to pursue a suspect, they must continue to do so until the suspect has been stopped.
b. Officers are not obligated to pursue vehicles at unsafe speeds.
c. No alternatives for high-speed chases exist when the suspect flees.
d. The safety of bystanders is not a consideration for officers when determining if a high-speed chase is the correct course of action.

Refer to the following for questions 78–79:

When an officer pulls over a driver suspected of driving under the influence, he or she will likely perform a field sobriety test. This starts with the officer asking the driver to exit his or her vehicle. There are three categories for field sobriety tests. A walk-and-turn test requires the driver to walk in a straight line, heel to toe, for nine steps and then turn and repeat the process in the opposite direction. The officer is looking for loss of balance that indicates the driver is under the influence of alcohol. The one-leg stand test also tests for loss of balance. In the one-leg stand test, suspects are asked to stand on one foot, raising the other six inches off the ground. The suspect will count until he or she is told to stop. Loss of balance or swaying indicates intoxication. A horizontal gaze nystagmus test uses the eyes to assess intoxication. During this test, officers will ask the suspect to follow a moving object with his or her eyes. If the suspect's eyes jerk or move in a pattern that is not smooth, it may indicate that he or she is intoxicated. Failing one of these three tests is enough probable cause for arrest in most cases. Drivers are not required to take field sobriety tests and cannot be forced to do so. Other factors, like the smell of alcohol coming from the driver and erratic driving, can also be enough probable cause for arrest under the suspicion of DUI. Officers may choose to breathalyze suspects on site if they have the proper equipment. While drivers may decline to take field sobriety tests, they are required to take a BAC test unless they wish to surrender their driving privileges. If they do not, officers will take suspects who failed sobriety tests to the nearest station to have their BAC tested.

78. Based on the preceding passage, which of the following statements is most accurate?

a. Suspects must fail all three field sobriety tests to be arrested on suspicion of DUI.
b. The horizontal gaze nystagmus test assesses a suspect's balance.
c. Even if a suspect passes all three tests, he or she can still be arrested on suspicion of DUI.
d. The walk-and-turn test requires suspects to walk the length of their vehicle before turning.

79. Based on the preceding passage, which of the following statements is most accurate?

a. Drivers who refuse to submit to BAC testing lose the privilege to operate a motor vehicle.
b. Field sobriety testing is mandatory for all drivers who are pulled over on suspicion of DUI.
c. Drivers may decline BAC testing in preference to other assessment methods.
d. By law, officers must allow suspects multiple attempts at the field sobriety tests.

Refer to the following for question 80:

Social media is growing in popularity and usage. This is something law enforcement officers can use to their advantage. Police departments can use social media as a communication tool. They can post community bulletins, alerts, and updates quickly in a way that reaches several people at once on their social media accounts. Social media may also be used in investigations. When suspects publicly post to their accounts, law enforcement can access that information without court authorization. This information can be used in investigations and entered as evidence. In instances where accounts and posts are private, law enforcement can utilize undercover profiles or informants to access information. In some cases, social media companies can be subpoenaed or ordered by the court to release information. This can include conversations that suspects had online and access to their usage data.

80. Based on the preceding passage, which of the following statements is most accurate?

a. A warrant must be obtained to access information that suspects post on social media.
b. Using social media to gather intel is a violation of a suspect's rights.
c. Social media companies can be required to provide information that is not public on a suspect's profile.
d. Police departments should not post information for the community to access on their social media.

Refer to the following for questions 81–82:

Artificial intelligence has the potential to be extremely useful in law enforcement. Using predictive analytics, AI can forecast crime, meaning it can predict crimes before they occur. This allows for departments to plan and allocate resources and funding appropriately. Facial recognition software can be used by agencies to comb through surveillance video and find suspects much quicker than doing so manually. For low quality video where faces cannot be recognized, AI can detect other qualities like the color of clothing or suspect height. AI is also used in gunshot detection and will soon be able to identify the exact location of a shooting, how many firearms were used, what kind of firearms were used, and how many total shots were fired. AI can also be used in a department's documentation process. It can transcribe audio from body cameras much quicker and more accurately than a human. AI is not intended to replace officers or humans in general, but it should be utilized to make the work humans do more efficient and accurate. Overall, it can be used to prevent crime, solve crimes more quickly, and create safer communities and neighborhoods.

81. Based on the preceding passage, which of the following statements is most accurate?

a. AI cannot be used with low quality surveillance video.
b. Officers use their own discretion when deciding to utilize AI.
c. Crime forecasting will allow money and manpower to be better assigned.
d. Utilizing AI in law enforcement will cut down on the number of officers needed.

82. Based on the preceding passage, which of the following statements is most accurate?

a. AI can cause more harm than good.
b. Gunshot detection abilities are still being developed.
c. Transcription of bodycam audio can be done more accurately by officers than AI.
d. AI does not play a role in community safety.

Cloze

The incident began (83) ____ Mary heard a suspicious noise in the middle of the (84) _____. There was a series (85) __ short, sharp bumps, and then her dog started barking. Except for the dog, Mary was (86) _____ in the house, so naturally she was on guard (87) ____ the start. Also, she had been having arguments (88) ____ her ex-husband recently, and she worried that he might (89) ____ been drinking. Her ex-husband's behavior could be erratic when he was (90) _____, and he had even been violent with her on occasion.

With this in mind, Mary decided to (91) ____ the police. She dialed 911 and the dispatcher (92) _____ her about the problems. (93) _____ Mary was on the phone, she (94) _____ the noise a few more times. She couldn't (95) __ sure, but it sounded (96) ____ it was getting closer. Her dog continued (97) __ bark. She gave the dispatcher her address and was told that an officer (98) _____ be at her house as (99) ____ as possible.

Mary (100) ____ up the phone. She called her (101) ___, who was still growling and barking in the direction of the front (102) ____, and brought him into the bedroom (103) ____ her. Then, she locked the door and huddled down (104) _____ the covers. She wasn't terrified; she was mainly hoping (105) ____ her ex-husband wouldn't make a scene that would wake the neighbors.

It took about ten minutes (106) ___ the police to arrive. During this period, Mary (107) _____ the suspicious noise a few more times. She thought that perhaps it (108) ___ getting louder, but she couldn't be certain. In (109) ___ case, she was pleased when she saw the flashing lights of the squad (110) ___ approaching and heard the front doorbell ring, even though the sound of the bell made her dog bark even (111) ____ furiously. She got out from under the covers and headed to the front (112) ____.

The officer who had responded (113) __ Mary's call asked her to describe the noise. When Mary did so, he (114) ____ that he had a hunch, pulled his large flashlight from his belt holster, and headed around the side of the (115)_____. About ten seconds (116) _____, he returned with a big grin. He asked Mary to come with him. When (117) ____ reached the side of the house, he shined his flashlight up at a large oak (118) ____. Mary could see that a large branch had broken and that the end of the (119) ______ was swinging from the base. When the wind caught the branch, it bumped against the upstairs window of Mary's (120) _____. Mary, a little embarrassed but (121) ____ very relieved, thanked the officer and went back (122) ____ her house, where she fell back asleep almost at once.

Reasoning

Instructions: Officers often face situations in which they need to determine how different pieces of information relate to one another. In this section, you will be presented with information such as a group or ordered series of facts, numbers, letters, or words. Your task is to study the various pieces of information and try to understand how they relate to one another.

123. Identify the next number in the series: 11, 22, 33, 11, 22...

a. 0
b. 11
c. 22
d. 33

124. Three of the following words are similar, while one is different. Select the one that is different.

a. Think
b. Ate
c. Jumped
d. Ran

125. Identify the next number in the series: 4, 8, 16, 32...

a. 36
b. 48
c. 64
d. 72

126. Three of the following things are similar, while one is different. Select the one that is different.

a. Hamster
b. Cat
c. Snake
d. Bear

127. Sandra received a 92 on the exam, and Terry's score was seven points lower. Victor scored ten points higher than Terry. What was Victor's score?

a. 75
b. 85
c. 92
d. 95

128. Wanda is twice as old as Ursula, and Ursula is seven years older than Vicky. How old is Vicky?

a. 12
b. 18
c. 22
d. Not enough information

129. Identify the next number in the series: 23, 44, 23, 54, 23, 64...

a. 23
b. 64
c. 74
d. 84

130. Three of the following words are similar, while one is different. Select the one that is different.

a. Sip
b. Gulp
c. Drink
d. Gnaw

131. Andrew, Ben, Carl, and Dan were in a race. Andrew finished after Ben but before Carl. Dan finished in between Carl and Andrew. Who won the race?

a. Andrew
b. Ben
c. Carl
d. Dan

Answer Key and Explanations for Test #4

Clarity

1. B: The other version fails to assign a verb to the second item in the list of things Pedro began his shift by doing, and thereby suggests that Pedro filled his service vehicle with a cup of coffee. In a list of this type, there must be appropriate verbs for each of the items.

2. A: The other version of the sentence is too wordy. Phrases like "at this point in time" and "along the lines of" make sense, but they inflate the sentence and make it more difficult for the reader. In the better version, "at this point in time" has been replaced by "now" and "along the lines of" has been replaced by "like," with no alteration in the meaning.

3. B: In the other version, it sounds as if the instructor rather than Leonard has received the diploma. The correct version makes this clear in the introductory clause. In addition, the incorrect version contains the wordy phrase "best student he had ever had," which can be expressed more precisely as "best student ever."

4. A: The other version is written as if the notebook was collecting the evidence. In the correct version, the subject is clear.

5. B: In the other version, it is impossible to tell whether sometimes refers to the guys in the locker room or the bragging. That is, the reader has no way of knowing whether the speaker sometimes saw these guys or they sometimes bragged about their cars. In the correct version, the meaning is plain.

6. A: The other version is incorrect because the word *but* is unnecessary and confusing. The introductory phrase begins with *although*, which alerts the reader that the main part of the sentence will describe something that has happened in spite of the district funding. Therefore, the inclusion of *but* at the beginning of the main clause is redundant.

7. A: The other version is too wordy. There is no reason to use the phrase *were resistant to* when the same meaning can be conveyed by *resisted.*

8. A: The other version contains a split infinitive, which is a common grammatical error that can lead to confusion. An infinitive is the verb form *to* ___. In sentence B, the infinitive is *to remain*. The placement of the phrase "if possible" breaks up the verb and makes the sentence more awkward. This split infinitive does not alter the meaning of the sentence, but there are situations in which a split infinitive changes the meaning from what the writer intends. Whenever possible, split infinitives should be avoided.

9. B: In the other version, it is unclear whether the speaker is an employee of the library or the speaker is doing some other kind of work there. The correct version makes this clear.

10. B: The other version of the sentence is confusing because the verb tenses are inconsistent. The first verb (*thought*) is in the past tense, and the next two (*remembers* and *returns*) are in the present tense. In the correct version, all of the verbs are in the past tense.

11. A: In the other version, there is a disagreement between the subject (*supervisor*) and the pronoun later used to refer to it (*they*). It is common in conversation to use they in this way, but it is grammatically incorrect and makes the sentence more confusing. In this sentence, where the subject is an undefined person, the pronouns *he* or *she* would be appropriate.

12. A: In the other version, the subject of the introductory clause is not identified until the end of the sentence. The correct version does a better job of presenting the same information.

13. B: In the other version, the word *where* is used incorrectly. Government oversight is not a place. It would be equally incorrect to begin the sentence with the phrase "Government oversight is when." The correct sentence expresses the same meaning more grammatically.

14. B: The other version of the sentence suggests that magazine journalists are more fair-minded than the newspapers themselves rather than the people who write for them. In the correct version, the terms of the comparison are clear.

15. B: The other version is unclear as to whether none of the cars were properly registered or not all of the cars were properly registered. In the correct version, the position of *not* makes the meaning plain.

16. B: In sentence A, the double negative "wouldn't never" is used. Not only is this wordy and awkward, but the two negatives cancel each other out to create a positive meaning that says he would break his oath.

17. A: The sentence states that the suspect is exclaiming his thoughts. The use of the word *yelled* in sentence B is redundant.

18. B: Sentence A contains a comma splice. Using the coordinating conjunction *so* corrects this.

Spelling

19. B: truly

20. A: mischief

21. B: reduction

22. C: candidate

23. C: camouflage

24. A: cartilage

25. B: official

26. A: guarantee

27. C: accumulate

28. D: business

29. A: especially

30. B: excel

31. A: science

32. C: fourth

33. A: labeled

34. A: category

35. C: liaison

36. C: margin

Vocabulary

37. A: *Irritate* has the closest meaning to *aggravate*. Both of these verbs mean to annoy or make uncomfortable.

38. B: *Correct* has the closest meaning to *rectify*. When *correct* is used as a verb, it and *rectify* both mean to set right, to make proper, or to straighten.

39. B: *Embarrass* has the closest meaning to *humiliate*. These verbs refer to making another person feel bad about himself or herself.

40. D: *Con* has the closest meaning to *bilk*. Both of them are verbs meaning to cheat or to take advantage of through trickery or persuasion.

41. A: *Recumbent* has the closest meaning to *supine*. Both of them mean lying down, usually on one's back.

42. D: *Lowering* has the closest meaning to *descent*. Both of these nouns refer to things that are decreasing in elevation or height, or which are getting lower in some other sense. For instance, a person who is beginning to adopt bad habits could be said to be in a descent.

43. B: *Overcome* has the closest meaning to *surmount*. Both of these words mean to triumph over or defeat.

44. A: *Distribute* has the closest meaning to *allocate*. Both of these verbs mean to spread things around or give things out over an area.

45. D: *Recovery* has the closest meaning to *redemption*. Both of these words describe the retaking of a good position after a down period.

46. D: *Reason* has the closest meaning to *rationale*. They both refer to the factors that influence an opinion or decision.

47. B: *Payment* has the closest meaning to *remuneration*. Both of these words refer to the compensation received for work that has been done.

48. A: *Replace* has the closest meaning to *supplant*. *Replace* and *supplant* are both verbs that mean to take the place of or to take over from.

49. C: *Accuser* has the closest meaning to *plaintiff*. Both of these words indicate a person who claims another person has committed a crime.

50. B: *Encourage* has the closest meaning to *incite*. Both of these words mean to spur on, push forward, or motivate.

51. D: *Verdict* has the closest meaning to *decision*. They both refer to choices made after thought or consideration.

52. D: *Clever* has the closest meaning to *cunning.* Both words mean to be crafty or calculating.

53. C: *Imitation* has the closest meaning to *simulated.* Both words mean a mockup, fake, or man-made version.

54. A: *Capable* has the closest meaning to *competent.* Both words mean able to do so.

Reading Comprehension

55. C: Based on the passage, the most accurate statement is that geographical data can be very useful in law enforcement. The last sentence of the first paragraph states that this data can be combined with police report data "to analyze where, how, and why crime occurs." The passage does not state that criminals are more likely to strike in open areas, but rather that the locations of these areas may affect crime. It seems more likely that criminals would avoid open areas. Finally, the passage does not state that police report data is useless without geographical data, but merely that these data sets can be usefully combined.

56. B: Based on the passage, the most accurate statement is that technological innovation has further increased the utility of geographic data. This is the main idea of the second paragraph. The passage suggests that geographic data has become more influential in recent years, but there is no indication that some geographic data has never been used before. The passage describes how geographic information systems have been used to inform police work, but it does not state that this work has lowered the crime rate. Moreover, there is no suggestion that the causes of crime can all be attributed to geographic factors.

57. A: Based on the passage, the most accurate statement is that public assistance is needed in the fight against terrorism. Indeed, most of the passage is a list of the things one should do to help combat this problem. There is no suggestion in the passage that other countries do not have effective counterterrorism organizations, or that civilians should not be near military facilities under any circumstances. Finally, the passage suggests that terrorists would be more interested in "places where large numbers of people gather," not unpopulated areas.

58. B: Based on the passage, the most accurate statement is that some activities are more suspicious when they occur in particular places. This is clear in the first sentence, which states that some activities indicate possible terrorist plans "especially when they occur" at certain spots. The passage does not state that every FBI field office contains a Joint Terrorism Task Force, but rather that every Joint Terrorism Task Force is located within an FBI field office. The passage never recommends that citizens try to apprehend suspects themselves. Also, the passage does not state that a large number of people tend to gather at utility stations, though it does include utilities in its list of "high-profile sites or places where large numbers of people gather." It seems more likely that a utility is an example of a high-profile site.

59. C: Based on the passage, the most accurate statement is that crime pattern theory focuses on the relationship between crime and place. The passage describes how certain crimes are more common in those places where they are easier to commit. The passage uses suburban burglaries as an example, but it does not suggest that the theory is only concerned with this area. Also, the passage does not place responsibility on the neighborhood watch, nor does it state that crime pattern theory only applies to minor offenses.

60. A: The passage states that crime pattern theory focuses on location and low guardianship. It then states that guardianship, such as social control, plays an important role in keeping crime at bay, so we can safely say option A is correct. Though the passage discusses the importance of social control, it does not state that crime always occurs when it is lacking, so option B is incorrect. Be careful of absolute statements like this that include words such as "always" and "never." Rarely is anything so definitely guaranteed. Similarly, the passage never guarantees that a high degree of social control will prevent crime, as option C suggests. Lastly, just because society plays an important role in stopping crime, it does not mean they play a larger role than law enforcement.

61. C: Based on the passage, the most accurate statement is that a footprint on a carpet would be an example of impression evidence. Impression evidence, according to the passage, is "created when two objects come in contact with enough force to cause an 'impression.'" The examples of pattern evidence are taken from shoes, but there is no suggestion that shoes are the most common source of this evidence. The passage does not state that either pattern or impression evidence is more valuable. Finally, it appears that these types of evidence must be examined and analyzed, but there is no indication that they need to be sent off to a state laboratory.

62. A: Based on the passage, the most accurate statement is that forensic examiners can match a shoe to a shoe print. This is described in the second paragraph. There is no suggestion that pattern evidence requires less analysis than impression evidence, or that a left shoe cannot be matched to a right shoe print. Finally, the passage does not suggest that a shoe print is not enough evidence to generate a conviction.

63. D: Based on the passage, the most accurate statement is that the broken windows theory draws a link between minor and major crimes. This theory suggests that areas in which there are many minor crimes will see a disintegration of the social order, which will lead to more major crimes. The broken windows theory would not explain crime in wealthy neighborhoods, since these areas are likely to be well-kept and free of "signs of disorder." The broken windows theory does not argue that vandalism is the worst crime, merely that it may contribute to a culture in which more serious crimes are likely to be committed. The passage does not state that the broken windows theory does not apply to rural areas. In fact, there is no reason to suspect that the theory would not apply there just as well.

64. D: Based on the passage, the most accurate statement is that departmental culture has far-reaching effects in law enforcement. This is evident throughout the passage. The second sentence of the passage asserts that departmental culture is closely tied to how officers interact with the public. It seems likely that the author of this passage would be in favor of departments receiving recommendations from the public, but this point is not made in the passage. Finally, the first sentence states that the primary factor influencing police behavior is the "management and culture" of the department, not the crime rate.

65. A: Based on the passage, the most accurate statement is that an organization should have defined values and principles. This is stated directly in the second sentence of the second paragraph. The passage never states that established policies can then be ignored. In fact, it lists "inspections and audits" as one of the priorities of a well-managed organization. The passage states that it is important to detect misconduct, but it never discusses how long this process lasts in general. Finally, the passage does not indicate that managers should receive preferential treatment. On the contrary, "equal treatment for all members of the organization" is listed as a priority.

66. A: Using the above coding system, the call number A-4-A would signify a drug offense in the northern part of the city during the day shift.

67. B: Using the above coding system, the call number B-0-B would signify a traffic violation in the central part of the city during the swing shift.

68. A: Based on the passage, the most accurate statement is that transnational crime often involves smuggling contraband across national borders. This is evident from the list of common transnational crimes given in the final sentence. The passage does not suggest that transnational crime is most common in Eastern Europe, or that it is restricted to the Internet. In fact, many of the crimes listed involve smuggling physical goods into other nations. Finally, transnational crime by definition is a problem for more nations than just the United States.

69. D: Based on the passage, the most accurate statement is that evidence does not have to be physical material. In the first sentence, evidence is defined as "information or objects." Evidence may be something like a bank record, which is more a piece of data than a material object. There is no suggestion that it is difficult to use dental history in a trial or that only the prosecution may introduce evidence during a trial. Furthermore, the passage suggests that evidence must be introduced in order to be considered by a jury.

70. B: Based on the passage, the most accurate statement is that teenagers and young adults are more likely than other people to be the victims of gun violence. This is stated directly in the third sentence. The passage does not state that young adults are more likely to commit acts of gun violence. Similarly, it makes no assertion about the leading cause of death among middle-aged citizens. In the last sentence, the passage states that most gun violence occurs "in cities and urban communities."

71. A: Based on the passage, the most accurate statement is that stress can be detrimental to an officer's performance. This is indicated in the final sentence, where it states that some officers with stress-induced fatigue "cannot properly protect themselves or citizens." The passage states that PTSD is associated with an inability to sleep, not excessive sleeping. It does not state that most law enforcement officers suffer from fatigue. The first sentence says that stress can lead to depression, but does not state the opposite.

72. D: Based on the passage, the most accurate statement is that stalking must include multiple episodes. According to the definition given in the second sentence, stalking requires "repeated (two or more occasions)" misconduct. Indeed, one of the key features of stalking is that it is a persistent pattern of threatening and/or unwanted behavior. Stalking does not require that the person be intending to stalk; On the contrary, the passage states that the definition of stalking only requires activities that would "cause a reasonable person fear.'" It is conceivable, then, that a person could be convicted of stalking without ever intending to cause fear. Stalking and domestic violence are not the same crime, in part because the latter requires proximity. Stalking, by contrast, may be perpetrated from a great distance, as in cases of cyberstalking.

73. B: Based on the passage, the most accurate statement is that sending a person flowers could be part of a pattern of stalking, if this is part of a pattern of menacing behavior. Specifically, the passage states that sending unwanted gifts can be a form of stalking. The passage does not assert that stalking must include verbal communication; on the contrary, the behavior may be limited to physical proximity or the posting of defamatory information on the Internet. The passage does not state that most stalking goes unreported by the victims. Finally, physical violence against another person goes beyond stalking and would be classified as assault.

74. C: Based on the passage, the most accurate statement is that Burglary always occurs at a residence, even when that residence is not a home. Indeed, the passage states that burglary may occur at vacation residences and hotels. The passage does not indicate how often burglary occurs at vacation residences. It does state that a vacation residence may be burglarized and that the occupant at the time is considered to be the resident. Similarly, burglary can occur at a hotel, with the resident defined as the person who has paid for the room at that time. Finally, the passage does not suggest that there are any situations in which burglary is lawful.

75. C: Based on the passage, the most accurate statement is that a burglary may be committed without a theft taking place. The second sentence of the passage states that "this crime usually, but not always, involves theft." Although the term *burglary* commonly is used interchangeably with *theft*, this passage defines burglary as merely the "unlawful or forcible entry or attempted entry of a residence." A burglary may not be committed where the person entering has a legal right to be present. The passage does not indicate whether a burglary without force is better than a burglary with force. One might guess that this is true, but it is not mentioned in the passage. Finally, breaking into a shed may be considered burglary, but only if the shed is located on premises owned by another person.

76. B: Based on the passage, the most accurate statement is that SROs have some responsibilities beyond those of their peers. The passage states that SROs serve as educators, mentors, and emergency managers. Those roles imply that SROs work directly with students, so choice A is incorrect. Unlike answer D claims, there is no comparison of the level of responsibility among officers in the passage.

77. B: Based on the passage, the most accurate statement is that officers are not obligated to pursue vehicles at unsafe speeds. The passage explains that officers should use their discretion when deciding to partake in a high-speed chase. Unlike choice A suggests, if a chase begins to exceed safe speeds, officers may choose to stop pursuing the suspect. Roadblocks set up along the suspect's route are a safer alternative to get suspects to stop, so the statement in choice C is incorrect. The safety of bystanders is taken into account when officers consider engaging in a high-speed chase, unlike choice D claims.

78. C: Based on the passage, the most accurate statement is that even if a suspect passes all three tests, they can still be arrested on suspicion of DUI. If probable cause exists outside of the tests, like the smell of alcohol coming from the driver or erratic driving, the suspect can be arrested. Only one test must be failed to be arrested, not all three like choice A states. The horizontal gaze nystagmus test assesses the suspect's ability to control eye movement, not their balance like choice B claims. The walk-and-turn test requires drivers to walk nine steps, not the length of their vehicle like choice D states.

79. A: Based on the passage, the most accurate statement is that drivers who refuse to submit to BAC testing lose the privilege to operate a motor vehicle. The passage states that suspects are required to take a BAC test unless they wish to surrender their driving privileges. It also states that suspects may decline field sobriety tests, unlike what is stated in choice B. Contrary to choice C, BAC testing cannot be declined due to preference for other testing methods, and the passage does not suggest this as a possibility. Choice D is incorrect because there is no mention of allowing suspects to take multiple attempts at sobriety tests.

80. C: Based on the passage, the most accurate statement is that social media companies can be required to provide information that is not public on a suspect's profile. The passage states that social media companies can be subpoenaed or ordered by the court to release information that is not available publicly. A warrant is not needed to access information that is accessible by the public online, contrary to what choice A states. The passage does not state or suggest that using social media is a violation of a suspect's rights like choice B claims. Choice D is incorrect because the passage does suggest that police departments can use social media to post information for the community.

81. C: Based on the passage, the most accurate statement is that crime forecasting will allow money and manpower to be better assigned. The passage states that it allows for departments to plan and allocate resources and funding appropriately. Contrary to what is stated in choice A, AI can be used on low quality video. It just can't be used to detect faces. Instead, AI detects other information, such as the color of clothes the suspect is wearing. The passage does not suggest that the use of AI is up to the discretion of officers as choice B argues. Unlike what choice D states, the passage states that AI is not intended to replace officers, but to make their work more efficient.

82. B: Based on the passage, the most accurate statement is that gunshot detection abilities are still being developed. The passage states that the technology used will soon be able to pinpoint the location of a shooting, how many firearms were used, what kind of firearms were used, and how many total shots were fired, implying it is still being developed. Contrary to choice A, there is no suggestion that using AI can be harmful. The passage does state that AI transcription is more accurate than human transcription, so choice C is incorrect. Choice D is incorrect because AI plays a role in community safety by helping to prevent and solve crime.

Cloze

83	when	**93**	While	**103**	with	**113**	to
84	night	**94**	heard	**104**	under	**114**	said
85	of	**95**	be	**105**	that	**115**	house
86	alone	**96**	like	**106**	for	**116**	later
87	from	**97**	to	**107**	heard	**117**	they
88	with	**98**	would	**108**	was	**118**	tree
89	have	**99**	soon	**109**	any	**119**	branch
90	drunk	**100**	hung	**110**	car	**120**	house
91	call	**101**	dog	**111**	more	**121**	also
92	asked	**102**	door	**112**	door	**122**	into

Reasoning

123. D: The next number in the series is 33. This pattern is just three recurring numbers: 11, 22, and 33. Therefore, 33 should follow 22.

124. A: The word *think* is not like the other three. *Ate*, *ran*, and *jumped* are all in the past tense, while *think* is in the present tense.

125. C: The next number in the series is 64. In this pattern, each successive number is twice the previous number.

126. C: A snake is not like the other three. Hamsters, cats, and bears are furry, but snakes are not.

127. D: Victor scored a 95 on the exam. If Sandra scored a 92 and Terry scored seven points lower, then Terry scored an 85. If Victor scored ten points higher than that, he would have scored a 95.

128. D: There is not enough information to solve this problem. Since no specific ages are given for any of the three girls, there is no way to use the information given to find a correct answer.

129. A: The next number in the series is 23. The pattern here is 23 followed by a number increasing by 10 each time. Since the previous term was 64, the next term will revert to the 23.

130. D: The word *gnaw* is not like the other three. *Sip*, *gulp*, and *drink* are all actions one would perform with a beverage, while gnawing is something one would do with food.

131. B: Ben won the race. If Andrew finished after Ben but before Carl, then Carl also finished after Ben. If Dan finished in between Carl and Andrew, then there is no chance he could have finished before Ben.

How to Overcome Test Anxiety

Just the thought of taking a test is enough to make most people a little nervous. A test is an important event that can have a long-term impact on your future, so it's important to take it seriously and it's natural to feel anxious about performing well. But just because anxiety is normal, that doesn't mean that it's helpful in test taking, or that you should simply accept it as part of your life. Anxiety can have a variety of effects. These effects can be mild, like making you feel slightly nervous, or severe, like blocking your ability to focus or remember even a simple detail.

If you experience test anxiety—whether severe or mild—it's important to know how to beat it. To discover this, first you need to understand what causes test anxiety.

Causes of Test Anxiety

While we often think of anxiety as an uncontrollable emotional state, it can actually be caused by simple, practical things. One of the most common causes of test anxiety is that a person does not feel adequately prepared for their test. This feeling can be the result of many different issues such as poor study habits or lack of organization, but the most common culprit is time management. Starting to study too late, failing to organize your study time to cover all of the material, or being distracted while you study will mean that you're not well prepared for the test. This may lead to cramming the night before, which will cause you to be physically and mentally exhausted for the test. Poor time management also contributes to feelings of stress, fear, and hopelessness as you realize you are not well prepared but don't know what to do about it.

Other times, test anxiety is not related to your preparation for the test but comes from unresolved fear. This may be a past failure on a test, or poor performance on tests in general. It may come from comparing yourself to others who seem to be performing better or from the stress of living up to expectations. Anxiety may be driven by fears of the future—how failure on this test would affect your educational and career goals. These fears are often completely irrational, but they can still negatively impact your test performance.

Elements of Test Anxiety

As mentioned earlier, test anxiety is considered to be an emotional state, but it has physical and mental components as well. Sometimes you may not even realize that you are suffering from test anxiety until you notice the physical symptoms. These can include trembling hands, rapid heartbeat, sweating, nausea, and tense muscles. Extreme anxiety may lead to fainting or vomiting. Obviously, any of these symptoms can have a negative impact on testing. It is important to recognize them as soon as they begin to occur so that you can address the problem before it damages your performance.

The mental components of test anxiety include trouble focusing and inability to remember learned information. During a test, your mind is on high alert, which can help you recall information and stay focused for an extended period of time. However, anxiety interferes with your mind's natural processes, causing you to blank out, even on the questions you know well. The strain of testing during anxiety makes it difficult to stay focused, especially on a test that may take several hours. Extreme anxiety can take a huge mental toll, making it difficult not only to recall test information but even to understand the test questions or pull your thoughts together.

Effects of Test Anxiety

Test anxiety is like a disease—if left untreated, it will get progressively worse. Anxiety leads to poor performance, and this reinforces the feelings of fear and failure, which in turn lead to poor performances on subsequent tests. It can grow from a mild nervousness to a crippling condition. If allowed to progress, test anxiety can have a big impact on your schooling, and consequently on your future.

Test anxiety can spread to other parts of your life. Anxiety on tests can become anxiety in any stressful situation, and blanking on a test can turn into panicking in a job situation. But fortunately, you don't have to let anxiety rule your testing and determine your grades. There are a number of relatively simple steps you can take to move past anxiety and function normally on a test and in the rest of life.

Physical Steps for Beating Test Anxiety

While test anxiety is a serious problem, the good news is that it can be overcome. It doesn't have to control your ability to think and remember information. While it may take time, you can begin taking steps today to beat anxiety.

Just as your first hint that you may be struggling with anxiety comes from the physical symptoms, the first step to treating it is also physical. Rest is crucial for having a clear, strong mind. If you are tired, it is much easier to give in to anxiety. But if you establish good sleep habits, your body and mind will be ready to perform optimally, without the strain of exhaustion. Additionally, sleeping well helps you to retain information better, so you're more likely to recall the answers when you see the test questions.

Getting good sleep means more than going to bed on time. It's important to allow your brain time to relax. Take study breaks from time to time so it doesn't get overworked, and don't study right before bed. Take time to rest your mind before trying to rest your body, or you may find it difficult to fall asleep.

Along with sleep, other aspects of physical health are important in preparing for a test. Good nutrition is vital for good brain function. Sugary foods and drinks may give a burst of energy but this burst is followed by a crash, both physically and emotionally. Instead, fuel your body with protein and vitamin-rich foods.

Also, drink plenty of water. Dehydration can lead to headaches and exhaustion, especially if your brain is already under stress from the rigors of the test. Particularly if your test is a long one, drink water during the breaks. And if possible, take an energy-boosting snack to eat between sections.

Along with sleep and diet, a third important part of physical health is exercise. Maintaining a steady workout schedule is helpful, but even taking 5-minute study breaks to walk can help get your blood pumping faster and clear your head. Exercise also releases endorphins, which contribute to a positive feeling and can help combat test anxiety.

When you nurture your physical health, you are also contributing to your mental health. If your body is healthy, your mind is much more likely to be healthy as well. So take time to rest, nourish your body with healthy food and water, and get moving as much as possible. Taking these physical steps will make you stronger and more able to take the mental steps necessary to overcome test anxiety.

Mental Steps for Beating Test Anxiety

Working on the mental side of test anxiety can be more challenging, but as with the physical side, there are clear steps you can take to overcome it. As mentioned earlier, test anxiety often stems from lack of preparation, so the obvious solution is to prepare for the test. Effective studying may be the most important weapon you have for beating test anxiety, but you can and should employ several other mental tools to combat fear.

First, boost your confidence by reminding yourself of past success—tests or projects that you aced. If you're putting as much effort into preparing for this test as you did for those, there's no reason you should expect to fail here. Work hard to prepare; then trust your preparation.

Second, surround yourself with encouraging people. It can be helpful to find a study group, but be sure that the people you're around will encourage a positive attitude. If you spend time with others who are anxious or cynical, this will only contribute to your own anxiety. Look for others who are motivated to study hard from a desire to succeed, not from a fear of failure.

Third, reward yourself. A test is physically and mentally tiring, even without anxiety, and it can be helpful to have something to look forward to. Plan an activity following the test, regardless of the outcome, such as going to a movie or getting ice cream.

When you are taking the test, if you find yourself beginning to feel anxious, remind yourself that you know the material. Visualize successfully completing the test. Then take a few deep, relaxing breaths and return to it. Work through the questions carefully but with confidence, knowing that you are capable of succeeding.

Developing a healthy mental approach to test taking will also aid in other areas of life. Test anxiety affects more than just the actual test—it can be damaging to your mental health and even contribute to depression. It's important to beat test anxiety before it becomes a problem for more than testing.

Study Strategy

Being prepared for the test is necessary to combat anxiety, but what does being prepared look like? You may study for hours on end and still not feel prepared. What you need is a strategy for test prep. The next few pages outline our recommended steps to help you plan out and conquer the challenge of preparation.

Step 1: Scope Out the Test

Learn everything you can about the format (multiple choice, essay, etc.) and what will be on the test. Gather any study materials, course outlines, or sample exams that may be available. Not only will this help you to prepare, but knowing what to expect can help to alleviate test anxiety.

Step 2: Map Out the Material

Look through the textbook or study guide and make note of how many chapters or sections it has. Then divide these over the time you have. For example, if a book has 15 chapters and you have five days to study, you need to cover three chapters each day. Even better, if you have the time, leave an extra day at the end for overall review after you have gone through the material in depth.

If time is limited, you may need to prioritize the material. Look through it and make note of which sections you think you already have a good grasp on, and which need review. While you are studying, skim quickly through the familiar sections and take more time on the challenging parts.

Write out your plan so you don't get lost as you go. Having a written plan also helps you feel more in control of the study, so anxiety is less likely to arise from feeling overwhelmed at the amount to cover.

Step 3: Gather Your Tools

Decide what study method works best for you. Do you prefer to highlight in the book as you study and then go back over the highlighted portions? Or do you type out notes of the important information? Or is it helpful to make flashcards that you can carry with you? Assemble the pens, index cards, highlighters, post-it notes, and any other materials you may need so you won't be distracted by getting up to find things while you study.

If you're having a hard time retaining the information or organizing your notes, experiment with different methods. For example, try color-coding by subject with colored pens, highlighters, or post-it notes. If you learn better by hearing, try recording yourself reading your notes so you can listen while in the car, working out, or simply sitting at your desk. Ask a friend to quiz you from your flashcards, or try teaching someone the material to solidify it in your mind.

Step 4: Create Your Environment

It's important to avoid distractions while you study. This includes both the obvious distractions like visitors and the subtle distractions like an uncomfortable chair (or a too-comfortable couch that makes you want to fall asleep). Set up the best study environment possible: good lighting and a comfortable work area. If background music helps you focus, you may want to turn it on, but otherwise keep the room quiet. If you are using a computer to take notes, be sure you don't have any other windows open, especially applications like social media, games, or anything else that could distract you. Silence your phone and turn off notifications. Be sure to keep water close by so you stay hydrated while you study (but avoid unhealthy drinks and snacks).

Also, take into account the best time of day to study. Are you freshest first thing in the morning? Try to set aside some time then to work through the material. Is your mind clearer in the afternoon or evening? Schedule your study session then. Another method is to study at the same time of day that you will take the test, so that your brain gets used to working on the material at that time and will be ready to focus at test time.

Step 5: Study!

Once you have done all the study preparation, it's time to settle into the actual studying. Sit down, take a few moments to settle your mind so you can focus, and begin to follow your study plan. Don't give in to distractions or let yourself procrastinate. This is your time to prepare so you'll be ready to fearlessly approach the test. Make the most of the time and stay focused.

Of course, you don't want to burn out. If you study too long you may find that you're not retaining the information very well. Take regular study breaks. For example, taking five minutes out of every hour to walk briskly, breathing deeply and swinging your arms, can help your mind stay fresh.

As you get to the end of each chapter or section, it's a good idea to do a quick review. Remind yourself of what you learned and work on any difficult parts. When you feel that you've mastered the material, move on to the next part. At the end of your study session, briefly skim through your notes again.

But while review is helpful, cramming last minute is NOT. If at all possible, work ahead so that you won't need to fit all your study into the last day. Cramming overloads your brain with more information than it can process and retain, and your tired mind may struggle to recall even previously learned information when it is overwhelmed with last-minute study. Also, the urgent nature of cramming and the stress placed on your brain contribute to anxiety. You'll be more likely to go to the test feeling unprepared and having trouble thinking clearly.

So don't cram, and don't stay up late before the test, even just to review your notes at a leisurely pace. Your brain needs rest more than it needs to go over the information again. In fact, plan to finish your studies by noon or early afternoon the day before the test. Give your brain the rest of the day to relax or focus on other things, and get a good night's sleep. Then you will be fresh for the test and better able to recall what you've studied.

Step 6: Take a Practice Test

Many courses offer sample tests, either online or in the study materials. This is an excellent resource to check whether you have mastered the material, as well as to prepare for the test format and environment.

Check the test format ahead of time: the number of questions, the type (multiple choice, free response, etc.), and the time limit. Then create a plan for working through them. For example, if you have 30 minutes to take a 60-question test, your limit is 30 seconds per question. Spend less time on the questions you know well so that you can take more time on the difficult ones.

If you have time to take several practice tests, take the first one open book, with no time limit. Work through the questions at your own pace and make sure you fully understand them. Gradually work up to taking a test under test conditions: sit at a desk with all study materials put away and set a timer. Pace yourself to make sure you finish the test with time to spare and go back to check your answers if you have time.

After each test, check your answers. On the questions you missed, be sure you understand why you missed them. Did you misread the question (tests can use tricky wording)? Did you forget the information? Or was it something you hadn't learned? Go back and study any shaky areas that the practice tests reveal.

Taking these tests not only helps with your grade, but also aids in combating test anxiety. If you're already used to the test conditions, you're less likely to worry about it, and working through tests until you're scoring well gives you a confidence boost. Go through the practice tests until you feel comfortable, and then you can go into the test knowing that you're ready for it.

Test Tips

On test day, you should be confident, knowing that you've prepared well and are ready to answer the questions. But aside from preparation, there are several test day strategies you can employ to maximize your performance.

First, as stated before, get a good night's sleep the night before the test (and for several nights before that, if possible). Go into the test with a fresh, alert mind rather than staying up late to study.

Try not to change too much about your normal routine on the day of the test. It's important to eat a nutritious breakfast, but if you normally don't eat breakfast at all, consider eating just a protein bar. If you're a coffee drinker, go ahead and have your normal coffee. Just make sure you time it so that the caffeine doesn't wear off right in the middle of your test. Avoid sugary beverages, and drink enough water to stay hydrated but not so much that you need a restroom break 10 minutes into the test. If your test isn't first thing in the morning, consider going for a walk or doing a light workout before the test to get your blood flowing.

Allow yourself enough time to get ready, and leave for the test with plenty of time to spare so you won't have the anxiety of scrambling to arrive in time. Another reason to be early is to select a good seat. It's helpful to sit away from doors and windows, which can be distracting. Find a good seat, get out your supplies, and settle your mind before the test begins.

When the test begins, start by going over the instructions carefully, even if you already know what to expect. Make sure you avoid any careless mistakes by following the directions.

Then begin working through the questions, pacing yourself as you've practiced. If you're not sure on an answer, don't spend too much time on it, and don't let it shake your confidence. Either skip it and come back later, or eliminate as many wrong answers as possible and guess among the remaining ones. Don't dwell on these questions as you continue—put them out of your mind and focus on what lies ahead.

Be sure to read all of the answer choices, even if you're sure the first one is the right answer. Sometimes you'll find a better one if you keep reading. But don't second-guess yourself if you do immediately know the answer. Your gut instinct is usually right. Don't let test anxiety rob you of the information you know.

If you have time at the end of the test (and if the test format allows), go back and review your answers. Be cautious about changing any, since your first instinct tends to be correct, but make sure you didn't misread any of the questions or accidentally mark the wrong answer choice. Look over any you skipped and make an educated guess.

At the end, leave the test feeling confident. You've done your best, so don't waste time worrying about your performance or wishing you could change anything. Instead, celebrate the successful completion of this test. And finally, use this test to learn how to deal with anxiety even better next time.

Review Video: Test Anxiety
Visit mometrix.com/academy and enter code: 100340

Important Qualification

Not all anxiety is created equal. If your test anxiety is causing major issues in your life beyond the classroom or testing center, or if you are experiencing troubling physical symptoms related to your anxiety, it may be a sign of a serious physiological or psychological condition. If this sounds like your situation, we strongly encourage you to seek professional help.

Additional Bonus Material

Due to our efforts to try to keep this book to a manageable length, we've created a link that will give you access to all of your additional bonus material:

mometrix.com/bonus948/pelletb

Printed in the USA
CPSIA information can be obtained
at www.ICGtesting.com
LVHW080048151124
796614LV00004B/95

* 9 7 8 1 5 1 6 7 1 0 6 1 4 *